LIVE, LOVE, FIGHT

LIVING FOR WHAT REALLY MATTERS

LIVE, LOVE, FIGHT

LIVING FOR WHAT REALLY MATTERS

Greg Laurie

This book is dedicated to the congregation
of Harvest Orange County that I have the
privilege of pastoring.

It was to them at our mid-week Bible study that
I first delivered these messages. These messages were a joy to preach
and I trust will impact the reader as they learn more about what God has
done for them, and in turn, what He wants them to do for Him!

CONTENTS

INTRODUCTION

When Hetty Green died in 1916, she was reportedly the richest woman in the United States, leaving an estate of more than $100 million. In addition to her great fortune, which would be upward of $4.3 billion by today's standards, Mrs. Green was known for her miserly ways.

She ate cold oatmeal every morning to avoid the expense of heating the water. She wore the same black dress in public, which was believed to be the only one she owned. When her son suffered a severe injury to his leg, she took so long searching for a free clinic that his leg had to be amputated because of advanced infection. And while debating the merits of skim milk versus whole milk, she was said to have hastened her own death due to apoplexy. Hetty Green lived like a pauper even though she was millionaire and, by today's standards, a billionaire.

Many Christians today are like Hetty Green. Despite the spiritual wealth God has given them, they go through life always struggling. They seem to have no spiritual power or resources to draw upon, when in fact they actually do. They have these resources, but they just don't know it. And even when they do know it, they don't act on it.

The book of Ephesians was written for Christians like this, Christians who might not realize how much God has done for them. Ephesians has been dubbed *The Believer's Bank* and *The Christian's Checkbook*. It talks a great deal about what the Lord has done for us. In chapters 1 through 3, we'll learn about our spiritual wealth and standing before God.

Ephesians teaches how to live as well. In this great epistle, the apostle Paul not only tells us about what God has done for us, but how to live full, productive, and effective Christian lives. He tells how to lay hold of what the Lord has given us and utilize it in our lives.

This is also a book that teaches us how to love. In Ephesians 5, Paul deals in-depth with the family. We usually reference this definitive chapter whenever we talk about the role of the family that is so vital in our culture.

Finally, it's a book that teaches us how to fight. In Ephesians 6, we'll learn about the spiritual warfare we are engaged in and the whole armor of God that every believer needs to put on and use.

Live, love, fight—that is what we must do as followers of Jesus Christ, and Ephesians shows us how.

PART 1

LIVE

1

YOUR SPIRITUAL RESOURCES

In Him we have redemption through His blood, the forgiveness of sins, according to the riches of His grace. (Ephesians 1:7)

During a visit to Ephesus, I made a purchase that I would later regret.

Once a significant city as a Roman provincial capital and a busy commercial port, Ephesus is filled with New Testament history. But it also was the headquarters for the cult of the false goddess Diana. The people of Ephesus made money selling artifacts of this goddess, and it was very profitable for them.

Today, you can still buy little idols of Diana there. For the sake of illustration, I bought one of those idols to use in an upcoming message. Then I put it into my bag and forgot about it. That is, until a few days later when I looked over at my granddaughters and saw them playing with that little Diana idol like it was a doll. Needless to say, I got rid of it.

The Ephesian believers lived in a place where idolatry was blatant. Not only that, there was massive sexual immorality. Christians in Ephesus were trying to live a godly life in an ungodly world.

It is not unlike our culture today.

Here in the twenty-first century, our idols might not be little goddesses called Diana, but we have them just the same. Sometimes they're cars. Sometimes they're our own bodies. Sometimes they're our careers or other people. We make idols out of a lot of things. Whatever it may look like, an idol is anyone or anything that takes the place of God in our lives.

When you board a plane and are waiting for it to take off, one of the things the flight attendants will tell you is that should the cabin lose pressure, an oxygen mask will drop down from the panel overhead. Before you assist anyone else, including children, you are to put on your own mask first. Why is that? If you don't have oxygen and can't breathe, you can't help anyone. Once you are able to breathe, you can help others who need your assistance.

The same is true in life. We can't help others fight the spiritual battle if we don't first have what we need in our own lives.

THE CHRISTIAN'S CHECKBOOK

The good news is that God's heavenly bank has no limitations or restrictions, so you don't have to be spiritually deprived, depleted, or defeated. God's heavenly resources are more than adequate to cover your past debts, all of your present liabilities, and all of your future needs. There is so much in your spiritual bank account that you couldn't spend it in one hundred lifetimes.

The word *riches* is used five times in the book of Ephesians. Paul speaks of "the riches of His grace" (1:7), "the riches of the glory of His inheritance" (1:18), "the exceeding riches of His grace" (2:7), "the unsearchable riches of Christ" (3:8), and "the riches of His glory" (3:16).

Also, we find the word *grace* twelve times, the word *glory* eight times, and the terms *fullness, filled up,* and *fills* six times. Paul uses the key phrase, "in Christ," six times.

Clearly, in Ephesians, we see that God has done a lot for us. Now let's check out the Christian's Checkbook:

> Paul, an apostle of Jesus Christ by the will of God, to the saints who are in Ephesus, and faithful in Christ Jesus: Grace to you and peace from God our Father and the Lord Jesus Christ.
>
> Blessed be the God and Father of our Lord Jesus Christ, who has blessed us with every spiritual blessing in the heavenly places in Christ, just as He chose us in Him before the foundation of the world, that we should be holy and without blame before Him in love, having predestined us to adoption as sons by Jesus Christ to Himself, according to the good pleasure of His will, to the praise of the glory of His grace, by which He made us accepted in the Beloved.
>
> In Him we have redemption through His blood, the forgiveness of sins, according to the riches of His grace. (1:1–7)

Paul wrote this epistle "to the saints who are in Ephesus." In some of the ancient manuscripts of the book of Ephesians, however, there is a blank space where Ephesus would be. Some believe that because of this blank space, this epistle was a circular letter, not only meant for the Ephesians but also for many churches. Certainly we are benefitting from it right now. You could just as easily say, "Paul, an apostle of Jesus Christ by the will of God to the saints who are at [insert the name of your church here]."

You could even personalize it and put in your name where the word *Ephesus* would be. It is God's letter to you, because the word *saint* is another word for believer. *Saint* is not a word to describe someone who has been acknowledged by the Catholic Church or who has performed certain miracles. A saint is a believer. So if you are a believer in Jesus Christ, then you are a saint. I am a saint. (But you don't have to call me Saint Gregory if you don't want to.)

THE CHRISTIAN'S CALLING

The apostle Paul, of course, was previously named Saul—Saul of Tarsus. He was a very religious man and was a member of the Jewish Sanhedrin. Saul of Tarsus presided over the death of the first martyr of the church, the courageous young Stephen. Saul of Tarsus went on a rampage against Christians, hunting down men and women, imprisoning them, and in some cases, executing them. He was a vicious killer.

Saul of Tarsus was named after the first king of Israel, who stood head and shoulders above everyone in the country. It was a great name for a Jewish man to have. But after Saul of Tarsus was converted, he didn't want to be called by that name anymore.

So Saul, whose name was associated with height, chose the name Paul, which means "little." It would be like someone known as Big John changing his name to Peewee. But Paul's smallness became the canvas for God's bigness.

Notice in verse 1 of Ephesians that Paul identified himself as "an apostle of Jesus Christ by the will of God." We often think of people like the apostle Paul, Peter, James, and John as the spiritual elite. Without question, they were singled out by God. But we must not forget they were ordinary men through whom God did extraordinary things. Every one of them had flaws.

Paul was an apostle *by the will of God.* God has called each one of us to do some work for Him. I'm Greg, a pastor by the will of God. But you could just as easily say, "Mary, a nurse *by the will of God,*" or "Steve, an architect *by the will of God,*" or "Jeremy, a police officer *by the will of God,*" or "Terri, an attorney *by the will of God.*" The highest calling of God is what God has called you to be.

For example, if you had chest pains, would you really want Greg, a pastor by the will of God, to help you? I would pray for you, but I couldn't help you with chest pains. You would want Jim, a cardiologist by the will of God. You need the right person in the right place.

Some might insist, "No, it's a higher calling to preach."

It isn't a higher calling; it's a different calling. And it wasn't a calling that I chose, by the way. I didn't aspire to become a preacher. All I ever wanted to do was to draw cartoons. Why would someone like me, who was a poor student in school and who never spoke publicly, be called to do this? I don't know why, but I do know that God called me to do it and started opening doors for me to preach. We are all called to do something.

THE CHRISTIAN'S SPIRITUAL GIFTS

God has placed a spiritual gift (or gifts) in your life. The apostle Paul wrote to the believers in Corinth, "There are different kinds of spiritual gifts, but the same Spirit is the source of them all. There are different kinds of service, but we serve the same Lord. God works in different ways, but it is the same God who does the work in all of us. A spiritual gift is given to each of us so we can help each other" (1 Corinthians 12:4–7 NLT).

So how do you know what your spiritual gifts are?

Sometimes other people will see them before you do. Someone may say to you, "I think you have a gift as a leader." Someone else might say you have a gift in another area.

One way to find out what you are good at is to first find out what you're not so good at. Sometimes one of the best ways to discover your gifting is to volunteer for everything. For example, let's say that you decide to help out in the children's ministry at your church. And let's just say that it doesn't go so well. So you decided to help out somewhere else. Then one day, you find your sweet spot. You think, *This is what God has gifted me to do.*

However, a spiritual gift is different from a talent. We have talents to do certain things. Some are artistic, some are musical, some are great with numbers, and some are great at fixing things. We have God-given talents, but we also have gifts of the Spirit. Pray about what yours may be.

The apostle Paul also said something surprising to the Corinthian believers about spiritual gifts: "No, much rather, those members of the body [of Christ] which seem to be weaker are necessary. And those members of the body which we think to be less honorable, on these we bestow greater honor" (verses 22–23). Often we don't notice the people who work behind the scenes. Take, for example, our own bodies. Our heart, liver, and mind don't get as much attention as our eyes or hands or voice because those are on display. Yet they are still vital for the function of the body. In the same way, each member of the body of Christ is essential. We all have a part to play.

THE CHRISTIAN'S SPIRITUAL BLESSINGS

What's more, God has given us resources that are at our disposal. Paul continues in Ephesians 1, "Blessed be the God and Father of our Lord Jesus Christ, who has blessed us with every spiritual blessing in the heavenly places in Christ" (verse 3).

Does this mean that all the things God has given us are in some cloud somewhere? Are they in some planet in a distant galaxy? No. It means they are in the unseen world of spiritual reality—the invisible world.

A Christian effectively lives in two worlds simultaneously. I live in this place, on this earth. Yet I am a citizen of Heaven as well. Because of this, I see things differently than other people see them. I realize that in a sense, this world is my home right now. But I will go to my heavenly home one day in the future. And that is a great comfort.

In another sense, I am in "the heavenlies." I am in the spiritual world. If God were to pull the veil back and allow us a glimpse into the spiritual realm, it would amaze us because we would see angels and demons. We would see the swirl of super-natural activity surrounding us every day.

We find an example of this in 2 Kings 6, where Elijah and his servant woke up to find the enemy surrounding their city. Panicked, the servant woke up the prophet and said, "What shall we do?" (verse 15).

But Elijah, probably wanting to get back to sleep, said, "Lord, I pray, open his eyes that he may see" (verse 17).

Suddenly the servant's eyes were opened, and he saw the supernatural world, with the angels of the Lord all around him. He realized that, just as Elijah had told him, "those who are with us are more than those who are with them" (verse 16).

We may not see the supernatural world. But trust me, it is there.

Let's also notice something else about Ephesians 1:3. Paul wrote, "God . . . *has blessed* us with every spiritual blessing in the heavenly places in Christ" (emphasis added). The King James Version of this verse says that God "hath blessed us," which means it is done. Past tense. Paul wasn't saying that one day God will bless us; he was saying God already has blessed us.

Imagine for a moment that your friend hands you a gift on your birthday. So you say, "What are you giving me for my birthday?"

"Well," your friend says, motioning to the gift, "why don't you open what I just gave you?"

"I just want to know what you're getting me."

"Are you kidding me? Just open the box!"

We can be that way as Christians. Many times we ask for something that God has already given us.

We say, "God, when are you going to give me this?"

Meanwhile, God is saying, "Newsflash! You have it! Check your balance. It's already there."

We may ask God to give us more love. Yet the Bible tells us, "The love of God has been poured out in our hearts by the Holy Spirit who was given to us" (Romans 5:5). It is already there. Don't pray for an emotion; just start loving.

That person—I get so upset when I see her! I need more love!

No, you need to do more loving things. Try doing something out of your comfort zone. Pay her a compliment. Do a favor for her. Do loving things and the emotions will catch up.

This is certainly true of marriage. Sometimes those husbands and wives, whom we love so much, start getting on our nerves.

The things that once drew a couple together, because opposites attract, now drive them crazy. But a strong and happy marriage is a result of obedience to God and His Word. For a marriage to be good, even fulfilling, it takes effort on behalf of both partners involved. Again, do loving things, and the emotions will follow.

Another thing we may ask God to give us is peace. Yet we already have it, because Jesus promised, "Peace I leave with you, My peace I give to you; not as the world gives do I give to you. Let not your heart be troubled, neither let it be afraid" (John 14:27).

Or, we might pray for happiness and joy. But Jesus said, "I have told you these things so that you will be filled with my joy. Yes, your joy will overflow!" (John 15:11 NLT).

We might ask God to give us strength, yet He reminds us that "[We] can do everything through Christ, who gives [us] strength" (Philippians 4:13 NLT).

The Bible promises us that "by his divine power, God has given us everything we need for living a godly life. We have received all of this by coming to know him, the one who called us to himself by means of his marvelous glory and excellence" (2 Peter 1:3 NLT).

As followers of Jesus Christ, we have all the peace, all the love, and all the power that we need. So take hold of it. Start using it today.

2

WHY GOD CHOSE YOU

In him we were also chosen, having been predestined
according to the plan of him who works out everything in
conformity with the purpose of his will.(Ephesians 1:11 NIV)

Predestination is a subject the church has been discussing and
debating for some two thousand years. As someone has said,
"Try to explain divine election, and you may lose your mind. Try
to explain it away, and you may lose your soul."

I like what the great evangelist D. L. Moody said about predestination: "The elect are the 'whosoever wills'; the non-elect
are the 'whosoever won'ts.'"[1]

You could put it this way: God predestines every person to
be saved. The Devil predestines, if you will, every person to be
damned. You cast the deciding vote for yourself. You decide
where you will spend eternity.

The good news is that once you make the decision to believe
in Jesus, you have confirmed that God chose you.

God chose you, however, before you chose Him. Jesus said,
"You did not choose Me, but I chose you" (John 15:16). Before
there was a planet called Earth, before there was a garden called
Eden, before there was a man named Adam and a woman named

15

Eve, God decided in the counsels of eternity to choose you (and to choose me).

That is what the apostle Paul was saying to the believers in Ephesus: "Even before he made the world, God loved us and chose us in Christ to be holy and without fault in his eyes. God decided in advance to adopt us into his own family by bringing us to himself through Jesus Christ. This is what he wanted to do, and it gave him great pleasure" (1:4–5 NLT).

The Lord chose us because He loves us.

WHY DID GOD CHOOSE US?

But why? What goodness or merit did God see in us that He would choose us to be His children? I hope you're not disappointed in the answer I am about to give you. The answer is there was no merit or goodness that caused God to choose us. All you need to know is that God chose you before you were even born.

According to C. H. Spurgeon, John Newton liked to tell the story about a woman who once said to him, "Ah! sir, it is a good thing God chose me before I was born, because if He had waited until afterward, He would have changed His mind."[2]

We can smile at that like Newton and Spurgeon did. But the truth is that God knew exactly who we would become. He knows our strengths as well as our weaknesses.

Imagine, for a moment, that one day you suddenly had the superpower, if you will, of knowing the future. What would you do?

Well, I would go down to the racetrack and bet a lot of money on the horse that I know will win.

What you're saying is that you would try to profit from it. You certainly would pick a winner. You wouldn't go down to the racetrack with your newly acquired foreknowledge of the future and say, "I'm going to choose a horse that is going to lose." You wouldn't do that. You would choose a winner.

God, knowing all things, chose you, and He chose me. Why? We don't know. Even though God knew we would fall short so many times, He still chose us.

And not only did God choose us, but according to verse 6 of Ephesians 1, "He made us accepted in the Beloved." This means that right now, as followers of Jesus, we stand before God completely acceptable. There is nothing we've done to earn it. But we're acceptable to God.

The other day I was listening to a song on a Christian radio station with the words, "It's your approval I long for. . . ."

I thought, *Why would I sing that? Christians don't have to long for the approval of God. We have the approval of God.* The Bible says so. He made us accepted in the Beloved. We are not merely forgiven and justified and cleansed of our sin; we have been received and loved by God Himself. It's because of His deep love for His own Son. Because His Son lives in us, we now have His favor.

We have God's approval because of what Christ did for us, not because of what we did for Christ.

In what we can describe as the true Lord's Prayer, Jesus, speaking of us as believers, said, "I am praying not only for these disciples but also for all who will ever believe in me through their message. . . . May they experience such perfect unity that the world will know that you sent me and that you love them as much as you love me" (John 17:20, 23 NLT). Did you catch that? God loves you as much as He loves Jesus Christ. Do you think the Father loves Jesus Christ? Of course He does. Jesus is His only begotten Son, His dearly beloved Son. And God loves you just as much because of what Jesus did for you.

On the cross, God the Father treated Jesus as though He had personally committed every sin committed by every person who would believe, even though He didn't commit any of them. This is called the doctrine of substitution. It means that God punished Jesus on the cross as though He had lived our lives. The Bible says, "But of Him you are in Christ Jesus, who became for us wisdom from God—and righteousness and sanctification and redemption" (1 Corinthians 1:30).

Jesus lived to the age of thirty-three while He was on this earth. Why thirty-three? Realistically, He could have accomplished everything He wanted to do over the weekend. So why thirty-three years? Answer: Because He came and lived the perfect life.

Can you imagine how hard it would have been to be one of Jesus' siblings? I can just picture Mary saying to His brothers, "Now, boys, why can't you be more like Jesus?"

"But Mom! He is . . . like perfect!"

Yes, Jesus was perfect. He lived a perfect life. He never sinned. A sinful thought never entered His mind. He passed every test. And because of that, now we are treated as though we have lived His perfect life.

A perfect life? I haven't even lived a perfect day. And I'm not sure I've lived a perfect hour without some kind of sin entering in, especially in my thoughts.

Yet God has put that righteousness into our account as though we've passed every test. He took our sins out and replaced them with Christ's righteousness.

In effect, God is saying, "When I see you, I see Jesus. I love Him, and I love you. We are related. You are my son. You are my daughter. That's the way it is."

Your heavenly Father looks at you with love. He looks at you with approval. He looks at you with acceptance.

We are accepted in the Beloved.

HOW DID GOD CHOOSE US?

"So how did God choose me?" someone might ask. "What was the basis for His choice?"

I don't have an answer for that particular question.

Some believe in what is called "irresistible grace." This is the idea that God chose you before you chose Him, and you are going to believe in Him, no matter what. It already has been settled and decided, and you couldn't even resist the grace and pull of God if you wanted to.

There are also those of the same persuasion who believe in what we might describe as "double predestination," meaning that God chose some people for Heaven and other people for hell, as though He says to one person, "I choose you for Heaven" while He says to another, "I choose you for hell."

I don't believe that.

I reject completely that God chooses certain people to go to hell. I think this contradicts what the Bible teaches, including verses such as 2 Peter 3:9, which says that God "is not willing that any should perish but that all should come to repentance."

Along these same lines, some believe in "limited atonement." That simply means that Christ only died for the elect, for those He chose ahead of time.

Personally, I don't believe in that, either.

I believe that Christ died for the *whole* world. I believe the grace of God *can be* resisted. That is why the Bible tells us not to resist the Holy Spirit, because He *can be* resisted. God has given us a free will. The Scriptures are clear in pointing out that God gives us a choice in the matter.

Of course, the definitive verse is John 3:16: "For God so loved *the world* that He gave His only begotten Son, that whoever believes in Him should not perish but have everlasting life" (emphasis added).

Notice this verse doesn't say, "For God so loved only the elect . . ." or "For God so loved the chosen ones."

Rather, it says that *whoever* believes in Him should not perish but have everlasting life. *Whoever*—not the elect who cannot resist His grace. *Whoever*. This is an open invitation to all of humanity. Whether we like it or not, the Bible teaches both predestination and free will.

Here is an illustration that I adapted from H.A. Ironside's commentary on Ephesians, "In the Heavenlies". Say you are cruising down the freeway of life, just going with the flow. You're empty. You're frustrated. You're alone. Then you notice an off-ramp. At the end of that little off-ramp, there is a building with a door. On the door there is a sign that says whosoever will, let him come.

You can see a couple of people pulling off, but most are charging ahead. Every day, you keep driving that freeway and keep noticing that off-ramp and the building with the door that says whosoever will, let him come. In fact, you've actually talked with people who have actually gone through that door, and they've told you how wonderful it is.

You think about doing what they did, but you're afraid. And then one day you think, *I'm just going to do it.* So you pull over, get out of your car, and open that door. As you step inside, the door closes behind you, and you turn around to look. There on the inside of the door is another sign, which says, chosen in Christ from the foundation of the world.

You chose.

But God chose too.

He chose you.

You chose Him. And you did have a choice in the matter. That is a glorious thing.

Maybe we don't understand it completely, but it is a reality we need to accept.

Yet some will say, "I think we need to be very careful. I don't think we can say 'God loves you' to nonbelievers, because if they are the nonelect then God doesn't really love them. If people pray to ask Christ into their heart, and they are not among the elect, we are giving them false assurance if we tell them Jesus came into their heart."

If we believe that, then how will we "go into all the world and preach the gospel to every creature," as Jesus commanded (Mark 16:15)? I don't know whom God has chosen. I don't know whom God hasn't chosen. But to again quote D. L. Moody, "Lord, save the elect—and then select some more!"[3]

I acknowledge that salvation is a work of God. There is nothing I can say to convince a person to believe in Jesus. I've had people ask me, "What is the one thing you can say to make a person believe?"

The answer is *nothing*. We evangelists don't carry a secret card that we pull out at just the right time, read it aloud, and have people suddenly come to faith. There is no such thing. I simply know that salvation is a work of the Holy Spirit.

Jesus said, "No one can come to me unless the Father who sent me draws them, and I will raise them up at the last day" (John 6:44 NIV). Salvation is up to God. Our job is to "tell others about Christ, warning everyone and teaching everyone with all the wisdom God has given us" (Colossians 1:28 NLT). It is our job to reach as many people as possible.

That is why Harvest Ministries does evangelistic crusades. We want to reach as many people as we possibly can in the shortest amount of time we can. That is our commission. That is what Christ has commanded us to do: go into all the world and preach the gospel.

When the apostle Paul preached in a place called Pisidian Antioch, the Bible tells us that "when the Gentiles heard this, they were glad and honored the word of the Lord; and *all who were appointed for eternal life believed*" (Acts 13:48 NIV, emphasis added).

I keep that in mind when I'm giving an invitation at the end of a message. Sometimes thousands have come forward after an invitation. And sometimes three people have responded. I simply remember that as many who are appointed for eternal life will believe. I leave it in God's hands. I believe that God's Spirit will do the things He wants to do.

We just need to do our part and let God do His. Romans 10:13 says that "everyone who calls on the name of the lord will be saved" (NLT). It is God who brings about conversion.

Paul reminds us of this in 1 Corinthians 3, where he wrote, "It's not important who does the planting, or who does the watering. What's important is that God makes the seed grow" (verse 7 NLT).

WHAT ARE WE CHOSEN FOR?

We talk a lot about the *why* of predestination. But I think something important we miss is the *what*—what did God predestine us for? We find the answer right here in the first chapter of Ephesians.

God Chose Us to Be Adopted into His Family

Look at verse 5: "He predestined us for adoption to sonship through Jesus Christ, in accordance with his pleasure and will" (NIV). God wants you to walk in fellowship, relationship, and friendship with Him. And God does this "in accordance with his pleasure and will," which means that He loves doing this.

He lovingly adopts us, as 1 John 3:1 says, "Behold what manner of love the Father has bestowed on us, that we should be called children of God." And Romans 8:15 tells us, "For you did not receive the spirit of bondage again to fear, but you received the Spirit of adoption by whom we cry out, 'Abba, Father.'" It is sort of like when I spend time with my grandchildren. I may buy them dinner. Then I might get them a dessert. Or, maybe I'll buy them a little toy. It isn't something I do out of a sense of duty. I love to be with them. It's my joy.

God feels the same way about us. Jesus said, "Do not fear, little flock, for it is your Father's good pleasure to give you the kingdom" (Luke 12:32 NIV). It's God's pleasure to do this.

God Chose Us to Be Holy and without Blame

In Ephesians 1:4, we see that "He chose us in Him before the foundation of the world, that we should be holy and without blame before Him in love." This is the outgrowth of our relationship with God.

You might say, "Well, God loves me the way that I am."

Yes, but He doesn't want to leave you that way.

"Holiness" speaks of our inward purity, while "without blame" speaks of our outward condition of purity. He wants us to have a pure heart. He wants us to be pure in our actions. If we really are Christians and know what it is to walk with Christ, then it should affect us in the things that we say, do, and even think.

You and I were like slaves on the open market. No one wanted us. They wouldn't pay full price, and they wouldn't pay half price, either. Then along came Jesus.

He took one look at us and said, "I choose you." And then He paid the price—*the full price.*

He motions to us and says, "Come on. We're going down to the courthouse."

"What are we going to do there?"

"Actually, I am going to adopt you."

"What?"

"I don't want you to be a slave like you were before," Jesus says. "You can serve Me voluntarily, but I want you to be My child. You can bear My name now, *Christian,* because you follow Me; I live in you."

Yet sometimes we mess up and sin as followers of Jesus, and we're ashamed. We might even feel as though we have lost our position: *I'm no longer His child. I'm not worthy.*

Newsflash: You never were worthy. And you never will be worthy. It isn't about that. It's about the fact that God loves you and chose you.

The more you know about God's love for you, the more you will grow in your love for Him. As 1 John 4:19 points out, "We love Him because He first loved us."

Perhaps one of the reasons we do so little for the Lord is because we don't realize how much He has done for us. We should be grateful for all that God has done for us.

God Chose Us so We Might Become More Like Jesus Every Day

Often we miss the big picture of Romans 8:28, which says, "And we know that all things work together for good to those who love God, to those who are the called according to His purpose." We forget that after Romans 8:28 comes Romans 8:29: "For whom He foreknew, He also predestined to be conformed to the image of His Son, that He might be the firstborn among many brethren."

When things happen in life that make no sense, we might say, "God, I don't know why this is happening, but Romans 8:28 says that 'all things work together for good to those who love God, to those who are the called according to His purpose.'" Then some time goes by, and we realize that the bad thing resulted in a good thing.

But then there are times in life when something really bad happens, and we don't see how it is working together for good. We don't see any good. We just see pain and more pain.

I know this from personal experience.

God's end game, so to speak, is not to make us happy; it's to make us holy. That is not to say God does not want you to be happy, for indeed He does. The great thing about it is that happiness is a by-product of holiness. If you live a holy life, then you will be a happy person. If you don't live a holy life, then you will be the unhappiest person around.

Are there things in your life that don't make sense? Maybe they will in a year or ten years. Or maybe they never will make sense this side of Heaven. But one day when you enter God's presence, it all will come into focus.

God chose you that you might be more like Jesus every day. Can people see that? It's a great compliment when someone says, "Man, you've changed! You're not the same person you used to be. You're like a whole new you!"

God's goal is to make you like Jesus.

God Chose Us so We Might Bear Spiritual Fruit

Jesus said, "You didn't choose me. I chose you. I appointed you to go and produce lasting fruit, so that the Father will give you whatever you ask for, using my name" (John 15:16 NLT). When someone is really walking with Christ, you will see spiritual fruit in their lives. According to Galatians 5, the fruit of the Spirit is "love, joy, peace, longsuffering, kindness, goodness, faithfulness, gentleness, self-control" (verses 22–23). If you are a follower of Jesus, those should be the earmarks of your life. People should be able to see these qualities in you. Again, Jesus said, "By their fruit you will recognize them" (Matthew 7:20 NIV).

If you know anything of God's choosing you and loving you, then it should cause you to want to live a holy life, bring honor and glory to His name, and bear spiritual fruit. God chose us so that we might live spiritually fruitful lives.

HOW DO WE KNOW IF WE'RE CHOSEN?

"But how do I know if I'm chosen?" someone might ask. I have the answer. Are you ready? It's very simple: Believe in Jesus Christ, and you have just proved that you were chosen. There is God's grace, but it can be resisted. There is God's offer of forgiveness, but it can be turned away. Now the ball is in your court. You cast the deciding vote.

Maybe you have gone to church for years, but you've never known how much God loved you or what God did for you. You can't remember a moment when you said, "Jesus, be my Savior and my Lord."

You can't live off someone else's relationship with God. You must come to Christ on your own and believe in Him.

Jesus showed His love for us by dying on the cross in our place and shedding His blood. Then He rose from the dead. He will come and live in your heart and life right now if you will ask Him in. He says, "Behold, I stand at the door and knock. If anyone hears My voice and opens the door, I will come in to him and dine with him, and he with Me" (Revelation 3:20).

Don't let someone else do your thinking for you. Think for yourself.

Get off that freeway leading to death. Get on that narrow road that leads to life. See the door that says whosoever will, let him come? That is for you.

3

PART OF THE FAMILY

In Him we have redemption through His blood, the forgiveness of sins, according to the riches of His grace. (Ephesians 1:7)

There has never been a single drop of blood that flowed through the veins of any man or woman in all of history that was like the blood of Jesus Christ. That is because Jesus was God. He was God in the manger as a helpless little baby. He was God as an adolescent. He was God as a young man. He was God at the cross. And He was God at the resurrection.

We can know God in a personal way and be adopted into His family because this redemption, this access, this relationship, comes through the blood that was shed by Jesus Christ. Verse 7 of Ephesians 1 tells us that "in Him we have redemption through His blood, the forgiveness of sins, according to the riches of His grace."

When we read in the Old Testament about the animal sacrifices that were brought to the tabernacle, and later to the temple, they were a prototype of things to come. When the priests would slay the animals on the altar and drain their blood, that was pointing to something greater. Ultimately, it was pointing to Jesus Christ, who, as the Lamb of God, would take upon Himself the sin of the world.

It's interesting that in the Old Testament, the word *atonement* means covering. Have you ever been eating out somewhere and spilled something on yourself? You might cover it up with something, but you haven't really dealt with the problem. That is what *atonement* means in the Old Testament.

But in the New Testament, *atonement* has a different meaning: *at-one-ment*. The Old Testament's atonement never could meet the righteous demands of God because we always will fall short and break those commandments. Atonement through Jesus Christ doesn't just cover up our sins; they are forgiven and removed. Through Jesus Christ, we come into a relationship with God. We are at one with Him—*at-one-ment*.

THE ISSUE OF WORTHINESS

The blood of Jesus was the blood of God, but it was human blood too. Jesus was fully God, yet He was fully human. He felt real pain. He shed real blood. And this blood, according to verse 6, makes us "accepted in the Beloved."

Have you ever noticed how false gods are always depicted as being angry? They always seem ticked off, don't they? People who worship them are always concerned about offending the gods and are always trying to appease them.

Sometimes we will bring that kind of thinking into our relationship with Christ. We think, *I was really good this week. I read my Bible every day and remembered to share my faith. I can go to church, and God will hear me.*

But at other times, we might think, *I messed up this week. I didn't read my Bible even once. I didn't tell anyone about God. In fact, a non-Christian told me never to talk to him about God. I can't go to church this week.*

Whether you're doing great as a Christian or doing poorly, we are accepted in the Beloved through the blood of Jesus Christ. Don't forget that. As Hebrews tells us, "We can boldly enter Heaven's Most Holy Place because of the blood of Jesus. By his death, Jesus opened a new and life-giving way through the curtain into the Most Holy Place" (10:19–20 NLT). The Devil always will attempt to drive you from the Cross, and the Holy Spirit will always draw you to it. When you have sinned, Satan will condemn you and drive you away. But the Holy Spirit will convict you and draw you in.

You may say, "But Greg, I am not worthy to approach God."

I am not saying that you are worthy to approach God, but I am saying that you *can* approach God. Your worthiness, so to speak, is based on the death of Jesus Christ on the cross. What you need to accept is the fact that you never were worthy. And you never will be worthy. So stop with the issue of worthiness. You never will get there. But you do have access to God through the blood of Jesus. You have been redeemed—even if you have stumbled and sinned.

When you sin against God, you don't cut off your relationship with Him. If my son does something wrong, he doesn't stop being my son. I may not be happy with him at the time, but he is still my son. Our relationship isn't severed.

However, communication can be severed.

HANGING UP ON GOD

When we sin against the Lord, it isn't as though He doesn't hear us anymore. Compare it to a phone conversation. We have effectively hung up on God. So we have to rectify that. The Bible says, "Listen! The lord's arm is not too weak to save you, nor is his ear too deaf to hear you call. It's your sins that have cut you off from God. Because of your sins, he has turned away and will not listen anymore" (Isaiah 59:1–2).

So if God turns away when we sin, how can we pray?

Let's say, for example, that a husband gets into an argument with his wife. It is really heated, and it's going on and on. The husband cannot come back to her a few minutes later and say, "When is dinner, by the way?"

That isn't going to work. He first has to go to her and apologize. Then he should let her cool down a little. It is only then that he can finally ask, "When is dinner?"

In the same way, before we come to God with all of our requests, we need to pray, "God, forgive me of my sin."

He will hear you if you pray that. But if you have been disobeying Him and carry on as though nothing has happened, He will turn away. He isn't going to answer your prayers. You are still His child, but communication has been broken. This good news is that it can be restored if you confess your sins.

Sometimes, as believers, we do things we shouldn't do. Some believers even will walk away from the church. Some walk away and have come back. And some walk away and never come back. Are those who never come back nonbelievers? I don't know. But I will say this: You can tell whether people are true Christians by where they wind up in the end. They may go astray for a long time, but eventually they will return.

My mother was a prodigal daughter for most of her adult years. It was only in the final days of her life that she recommitted her life to Christ. But she did believe, and she did return.

A SIGN THAT HE LOVES US

We are told in 1 John, "They went out from us, but they did not really belong to us. For if they had belonged to us, they would have remained with us; but their going showed that none of them belonged to us" (2:19 NIV). When you sin as a Christian, the Lord will chasten you. The Bible tells us, "The lord disciplines those he loves, and he punishes each one he accepts as his child" (Hebrews 12:6 NLT). That discipline, or chastening, as the New King James Version calls it, is a sign that He loves you. God doesn't discipline someone who isn't His child; He only disciplines His own children.

Have you ever been in a store when some child was throwing a tantrum? Maybe you've thought, *I would like to go over there and take care of that.* You can't do that, of course. In fact, you'd better leave it alone, unless you want the parent and child to turn on you right there in the cereal aisle. It isn't your privilege or right to disciple someone else's child.

In the same way, God only disciplines His children. So if you begin to stray, if you start to think an impure thought or do an unkind thing and suddenly feel guilt and remorse, that's good. God just gave you a kiss in the form of a little swat. He is saying, "I love you and don't want you to go that way. Go back over there. Listen to Me. I care about you." And that is a good thing.

So does God punish us as Christians? Let me put it this way: God disciplines Christians and punishes nonbelievers.

A non-Christian might say, "Hey, I don't know if I want to become a Christian. God will discipline me. I'd rather just do whatever I want."

You can do that. But you face the consequences. You'll be punished for your sin.

How bad is it? How does death sound? The Bible says "the wages of sin is death" (Romans 6:23 NLT). It is not just physical death, because everyone will physically die. It is eternal separation from God.

God does not punish His children because He put His punishment on Jesus Christ. Those who have put their faith in Jesus Christ don't have to face it. Isaiah 53 says, "But he was pierced for our transgressions, he was crushed for our iniquities; the punishment that brought us peace was on him, and by his wounds we are healed" (verse 5 NIV).

THE SEAL OF OWNERSHIP

God has redeemed you. He has adopted you into His family. He has given you access to His throne. And so you can be certain that He means business, He gives you a down payment, like a preview of coming attractions.

For example, when you go to a movie and sit through all the trailers, you're making an evaluation of upcoming films. You decide which ones you want to see—and which ones you don't. Then you go see the movie and find out the trailer was better. All the best parts were in the trailer.

God is saying, "This is a preview of coming attractions to let you know that I mean this. I have sealed you with the Holy Spirit of promise."

Long before there was FedEx and Amazon.com, there was an ancient way of sending merchandise. Goods being shipped from one place to another would be stamped with a wax seal and imprinted with a signet ring, bearing a unique mark of ownership. That seal meant, "Don't tamper with this item. It belongs to someone important."

The same was true of important documents sent by a king. They would be sealed with wax and imprinted with the royal seal. To open the seal would be defying the king himself.

God has put His royal seal on you as a follower of Jesus Christ. Maybe you don't see it. But God does. Guess who else sees it? The Devil. And he respects it. The Bible says that "even the demons believe—and tremble!" (James 2:19). The Devil knows when he is outgunned.

Not only is the Holy Spirit the seal of ownership that God has given to each of us, but according to verse 14 of Ephesians 1, "The Spirit is God's guarantee that he will give us the inheritance he promised and that he has purchased us to be his own people. He did this so we would praise and glorify him" (NLT). This word *guarantee* used here was used by the Greeks as a term for an engagement ring. When a guy proposes to his girlfriend, he has to demonstrate that he really loves her. A pair of shoes isn't going to do it. (Although some women might say, "What kind of shoes are we talking about here? Really good shoes might buy him a week.") No, what he needs to do is put a ring on it. He needs to show that he's serious.

Or, let's say, for example, that you want to buy a car. Would you go down to the dealership and say, "I'll take this car," get in it, and drive away? No, you wouldn't—unless you want to get arrested.

Instead, you have to fill out about 300 pages of paperwork, and then you have to show how serious you are by putting money on the table. Then you complete the transaction. Finally, they give you the keys so you can drive your new car off the lot, which becomes half of what it was worth five minutes earlier.

God is saying, "Okay, here's what I'm going to do for you. One day you will be in Heaven. One day all your sins will be forgiven and forgotten. One day you will be in a perfected body. But because I want you to know that I mean business, I'm going to put down a deposit in your life."

That deposit is the Holy Spirit.

Let's say for an illustration that there wasn't a Heaven, and all there was of the Christian life was a relationship with Jesus Christ. That's it—no afterlife, no future reward. Would you be a Christian for that alone? To me, it is more than good enough.

But of course there is a Heaven as well.

God is saying, "I'm going to give you Heaven. I'm going to give you glory. I'm going to give you perfection. But until that day, I'm going to give you the Holy Spirit so you will know that I mean business."

David prayed, "O God, You are my God; early will I seek You; my soul thirsts for You; my flesh longs for You in a dry and thirsty land where there is no water. So I have looked for You in the sanctuary, to see Your power and Your glory" (Psalm 63:1–2).

David was saying, "Lord, I saw you in the temple, but I want to see you that way all of the time."

Maybe you're thinking, *I want that. I want to have sweet fellowship with God all the time.*

The good news is God wants that too.

Why? Because you are signed, sealed, and delivered. You are chosen, adopted, redeemed, and sealed with the Holy Spirit.

PAUL'S PRAYER

At the end of Ephesians 1, Paul closes with a beautiful prayer for the Ephesians, a prayer with three movements. (If you're ever wondering how to pray for someone, start here.)

First, Paul prays for their enlightenment:

> For this reason, ever since I heard about your faith in the Lord Jesus and your love for all God's people, I have not stopped giving thanks for you, remembering you in my prayers. I keep asking that the God of our Lord Jesus Christ, the glorious Father, may give you the Spirit of wisdom and revelation, so that you may know him better. I pray that the eyes of your heart may be enlightened. (verses 15–18 NIV)

When Paul used the word *heart,* he wasn't only speaking of emotions. In our culture, we use the word *heart* to usually refer to how we feel. But in the Jewish culture, and more to the point, in the Bible, the heart speaks not only of the emotions, but also of the mind and the will.

Paul was saying, "I pray that you would have your eyes opened in your mind, in your heart, and in your will, and that you would see God's glory."

Have you ever been reading the Bible and had an idea come to life for you? It's as though God is speaking directly to you through that verse in the Bible. That is having the eyes of your heart opened.

Next, Paul prayed they would know the riches God had blessed them with: "I pray that the eyes of your heart may be enlightened in order that you may know the hope to which he has called you, the riches of his glorious inheritance in his holy people" (verse

18 NIV). Paul wasn't speaking of financial riches but of spiritual wealth. This phrase is not referring to our inheritance in Christ, as vast as that is. It is referring to His inheritance in us.

When God looks at us, He is thinking, "You are my greatest treasure. You are the most valuable thing that I have. I love you so much."

He looks at us with eyes of love. God sees us for what we are going to be, not just for what we are.

My grandkids all have such distinct personalities. I wonder what they will be like when they grow up. I see little glimpses here and there as they get older. Sometimes I think I have a sense of what they will be like.

But God, with complete foreknowledge, knows exactly what we will be. He looks at us in that way. God deals with us on the basis of our future and not on our past.

Michelangelo once said, "I saw the angel in the marble and carved until I set him free." We just see a chunk of rock, but God already sees His finished work, and He is chipping away.

Throughout our lives, we are chipped at. Things happen that don't make sense to us. But God sees what He will make you into. You are His inheritance. Paul was saying, "I'm praying you get that. I'm praying you see how much you are loved by God."

Last, Paul prays for power: "That you may know the hope to which he has called you, the riches of his glorious inheritance in his holy people, and his incomparably great power for us who believe. That power is the same as the mighty strength he exerted when he raised Christ from the dead and seated him at his right hand in the heavenly realms" (verses 18–20 NIV). Paul was saying, "I want you to know you have unlimited power to reach your objectives in Christ."

Our power to live the Christian life is a result of being plugged in. If you've ever had trouble with your television or computer and have called a help line, then you probably know the two questions they begin with: (1) Is it plugged in? and (2) Is it turned on?

We need to be plugged in spiritually. We plug in through prayer. We plug in through Bible study. We plug in through fellowship by being part of the church. It isn't like running on batteries.

I think some people think they can come to church, get charged up, and then make it through the week. It doesn't work that way. We need to be plugged in all the time.

Paul was saying, "I hope you see how much power is there for you right now."

We have all of the power we need. In fact, we have more power than we need. We just need to lay hold of it. We need to appropriate it. We need to start using it. God wants us plugged in all the time. We don't have to be in church to do it. We can be plugged into Him anywhere as we walk in fellowship with Him every day.

So plug in and walk in this fellowship with God. And remember this: He loves you as much as He loves His Son, Jesus Christ. Jesus prayed to the Father, "You have sent Me, and have loved them as You have loved Me" (John 17:23).

We would never doubt that the Father loves His Son. But we have a hard time wrapping our minds around the idea that God loves us at all. He doesn't just love us; He loves us as much as He loves Jesus. Because of the death of Jesus that satisfied the righteous demands of the Father, you and I have been made accepted in the Beloved.

4

YOUR PAST, PRESENT, AND FUTURE

And God raised us up with Christ and seated us with him in the heavenly realms in Christ Jesus, in order that in the coming ages he might show the incomparable riches of his grace, expressed in his kindness to us in Christ Jesus.(Ephesians 2:6–7 NIV)

I like fortune cookies. Not only do I like the way they taste, but I also happen to enjoy the funny little sayings they contain. Here are some actual quotes from so-called fortunes people have found inside these cookies:

> You will be hungry again in one hour. (That one is true for sure.)

> The fortune you seek is in another cookie.

> If you think we're going to sum up your whole life on this little bit of paper, you're crazy.

> Help! I am being held hostage in a Chinese bakery.

From time to time, we all wonder about the future. And maybe some people are even desperate enough to look inside a fortune cookie for help. But if you are a Christian reading this today, then I know your future. And I know your past too. I also know quite a bit about your present. And I don't have to know details about what you used to do or what your particular life-style was.

Greg, you're losing your mind, you might be thinking.

No, not really. I've simply read the second chapter of Ephesians. There we find the past, present, and future of every believer.

But I do know some things about you because the Bible says they are true of every believer in Jesus Christ.

YOUR PAST

First, there is your past:

> And you He made alive, who were dead in tres-passes and sins, in which you once walked ac-cording to the course of this world, according to the prince of the power of the air, the spirit who now works in the sons of disobedience, among whom also we all once conducted ourselves in the lusts of our flesh, fulfilling the desires of the flesh and of the mind, and were by nature children of wrath, just as the others. (verses 1–3)

It isn't hard for us to believe that certain people in this world are wicked. We know, for example, that ISIS is a group of very wicked people. We know that a serial killer is wicked. We know that a rapist is wicked. It is easy to accept these facts.

However, it is hard for us to think of ourselves as wicked. We cut ourselves a lot more slack than we do others. Have you ever noticed, for example, how you can be so short-tempered with someone else who is doing something that you often do yourself? We think we're a little—if not a lot—better than others. But guess what? God doesn't see it that way.

Spiritually Dead

When we live in sin, we're spiritually dead. The Bible tells us that "the wages of sin is death" (Romans 6:23), and "the soul who sins shall die" (Ezekiel 18:20). Everyone who does not know Jesus Christ is dead in their sins.

That's difficult for us to wrap our minds around because we know nice people who aren't Christians. They have bubbly personalities. They are fun to be with. They are outgoing. Maybe they are even caring and considerate. We may look at someone and think, *There is no way she is dead in her sins.*

Some people are closer to coming to Christ than others are, but if they are not believers yet, the Bible says they are still spiritually dead.

Non-Christians can't understand truths from God's Spirit. These things sounds foolish to them. They don't have the capacity to understand them (see 1 Corinthians 2:14). That's why Jesus said to the great religious leader Nicodemus, "You must be born again. You need to have a spiritual rebirth."

The good parent, the loving spouse, the honest worker, the caring humanitarian—they all need Jesus to save them, just as much as the drug addict, the drunk, the thief, the prostitute, or the terrorist. That is not to say they all live equally sinful lives. But it is to say they are equally in a state of sin and equally separated from God and from spiritual life.

The Bible acknowledges that nonbelievers are capable of doing good things. I would even say some of them are "good people" comparatively. They are good people in a broad sense. Jesus even said, "And if you do good to those who are good to you, what credit is that to you? Even sinners do that" (Luke 6:33 NIV). Jesus acknowledged there are people who do good things for one another. But that doesn't make you a Christian.

Jesus also said, "If you sinful people know how to give good gifts to your children, how much more will your heavenly Father give the Holy Spirit to those who ask him" (Luke 11:13 NLT). Jesus was pointing out there are parents who give good gifts to their children, but they aren't necessarily believers.

So, in a broad sense, there are good people who do good things. The problem is, they aren't good enough—because they aren't perfect.

Falling Short

When the Bible says we miss the mark, or we sin, it means that we fall short of God's standards. God wants us to be perfect. Yes, perfect. Jesus said, "But you are to be perfect, even as your Father in heaven is perfect" (Matthew 5:48 NLT). Have you lived up to that standard? No, and neither have I. We've missed the mark.

Everyone without Christ is dead in sin.

You see, we are not sinners because we sin; we sin because we are sinners. It comes naturally to us. We were all born with it.

I never had to teach my two sons to be selfish. They were born that way, just as I was born that way and you were born that way.

Notice that verse 1 of Ephesians 2 says, "And you He made alive, who were dead in trespasses and sins." You once were dead in your sins, and so was I. But God made *you* alive. He made *me* alive.

The word *trespass* means to cross a line. If you cross that line, if you cross over that fence, you are officially trespassing. In the context of the Scriptures, it means to break a commandment. If we lie, if we steal, if we take the Lord's name in vain, then we've committed a trespass.

Sins of Commission and Omission

So why didn't the apostle Paul just use the word *sin* here? Because it carries a different meaning from *trespass*. The word *sin* is translated from the Greek word *hamartia*, which means "to miss the mark." It's a term used in archery that refers to missing or falling short of a goal or a standard. In the spiritual realm, we fall short of God's standard of holiness. In the New Testament, this term for sin is used 173 times. In fact, it's the most common term used to describe sin.

There are different kinds of sin.

There is a sin of commission, effectively a trespass, which is to do what you should not do.

A sin of omission is not doing what you should do.

Someone might say, "I don't really think I sinned today. I can't remember lying or having an impure thought."

Maybe you didn't commit a sin of commission (although that is highly doubtful). However, let's just say, for the sake of a point, that you didn't.

But what about the sin of omission? The Bible says, "Remember, it is sin to know what you ought to do and then not do it" (James 4:17 NLT).

It works like this. Maybe God spoke to your heart and said, "Why don't you open My Word right now?"

You respond, *Lord, I'm updating my Instagram.*

Or maybe He nudged you to go talk to a certain individual.

I can't. I'm so busy. I have to get to work.

If you fail to respond to the Holy Spirit's leading, that could be a sin of omission.

The Bible says that if you say you have no sin, you're deceiving yourself (see 1 John 1:8). Whether our sins are intentional or unintentional, the result is the same: we are dead in our trespasses and sins.

That was the bad news.

But God...

Now comes the good news:

> But God, who is rich in mercy, because of His
> great love with which He loved us, even when we
> were dead in trespasses, made us alive together
> with Christ (by grace you have been saved).
> (Ephesians 2:4–5)

I love those two words: *But God.* Know this: God will always have the last word. Whether things are going well for you right now or whether they are going badly (and you wonder whether they ever will stop going badly), God will have the last word. There will be a *but God* moment for you.

I'm reminded of Joseph, who was so cruelly treated by his jealous brothers. You probably know the story. They sold him as a slave, and he went through a lot of twists and turns. He was falsely accused of rape and sent to a prison, where he was known to interpret dreams. Eventually word reached the king about Joseph's ability. So Joseph was taken out of prison and brought before the king. Joseph interpreted the dream that had troubled the king, and as a result, he became the second most powerful man in Egypt.

Then one day his brothers arrived in search of food because a famine had swept the land. Guess who was in charge of the food supply? Joseph. But he looked different. Maybe his head was shaved in the way of the Egyptians. Maybe he was wearing eyeliner. Whatever it was, his own brothers didn't recognize him. It had been years. In fact, they thought Joseph was dead.

When Joseph revealed to them who he was, they were terrified because they thought their lives were over.

Then Joseph told them, "But as for you, you meant evil against me; *but God* meant it for good, in order to bring it about as it is this day, to save many people alive" (Genesis 50:20, emphasis added).

But God . . .

Maybe you're experiencing some type of hardship right now. Something has happened that doesn't make sense to you. Perhaps you just were let go at work, or there is trouble in another area of your life. You wonder what's happening.

Or maybe you're sick. You just got the test results back from the doctor, and it's looking bleak. Maybe it's a friend or relative of yours who is deathly ill. Doctors have given them no hope. Paul wrote of his dear friend Epaphroditus, "And he certainly was ill; in fact, he almost died. *But God* had mercy on him—and also on me, so that I would not have one sorrow after another" (Philippians 2:27 NLT, emphasis added). *But God*...There will be a *but God* moment for you, just like there was for Joseph. God will intervene.

Others might find themselves in a difficult situation because they sinned against God. Take Jonah and the people of Nineveh, for example. Although Jonah preached to the Ninevites and warned them to repent, he still wanted God to judge them—and he thought that was what God would do.

In fact, Jonah had pulled up a front-row seat. The Lord caused a plant to grow over Jonah, and he sat in the shade, kicking back, waiting for God's judgment to rain on Nineveh.

Then we read, "*But God* also arranged for a worm! The next morning at dawn the worm ate through the stem of the plant so that it withered away" (Jonah 4:7 NLT, emphasis added).

But God...

Jonah's heart was in the wrong place. He wanted God to judge these people. *But God* messed up his little party.

Then there are the nonbelievers who have rejected God their entire lives. They have lived for themselves. They have amassed a great deal of wealth, like the man Jesus spoke of who had so much stuff that he had no room for it.

The man said to himself, "My friend, you have enough stored away for years to come. Now take it easy! Eat, drink, and be merry!" (Luke 12:19).

People still say that today: *Take it easy!*

Then we read, *"But God* said to him, 'You fool! You will die this very night. Then who will get everything you worked for?'" (verse 20 NLT, emphasis added).

But God . . .

God always will have the last word.

Coming back to verses 4–5 of Ephesians 2, "But God, who is rich in mercy, because of His great love with which He loved us, even when we were dead in trespasses, made us alive together with Christ (by grace you have been saved)."

That is your past.

YOUR PRESENT

Now let's look at your present:

> Even though we were dead because of our sins,
> he gave us life when he raised Christ from the
> dead. (It is only by God's grace that you have
> been saved!) For he raised us from the dead along
> with Christ and seated us with him in the heavenly
> realms because we are united with Christ Jesus.
> (verses 5–6 NLT)

Where is Christ right now? The Bible tells us that Christ is "seated . . . in the place of honor at God's right hand in the heavenly realms. Now he is far above any ruler or authority or power or leader or anything else—not only in this world but also in the world to come" (Ephesians 1:20–21 NLT). Jesus is above everything. He is above world leaders.

He is above the Devil. He is above demons. He is above everyone and everything.

That is great for Jesus, you might be thinking, *but what does that have to do with me?*

If you are a follower of Jesus Christ, it has *everything* to do with you because you are seated with Jesus. You are there with Him.

You see, there are things that are *positionally* true that are not *experientially* true. For example, the Bible teaches that you are saved and are going to Heaven. Are you in Heaven yet? No. Positionally, you know there is a place prepared for you in Heaven. And one day you will know experientially what you now only know positionally.

This doesn't mean you're immune from temptation or attack. But it does mean you're not a victim of the Devil. If you yield to Jesus, then you don't have to live a life of constant spiritual defeat. Some people are always down and always messing up week after week. They feel as though they need to "get saved" again and again. But a Christian doesn't need to get saved repeatedly. You have been saved. Now start acting like a saved person and take hold of the power that God has given you.

I'm not saying that you will be perfect as a Christian—far from it. But you can grow and experience strength that you never knew was possible in your life.

Of course, the Devil doesn't want you to know that you are seated with Jesus. He rather would have you think that he is God's equal and can pick Christians off at will. He doesn't want us to know that we have a wealth of spiritual resources to draw upon. He wants us to simply surrender, to pull out the white flag and say, "Okay, Devil, you win!"

We *can* resist temptation. And according to Ephesians, we have incredible resources to draw from. When you are tempted, you can walk away. When you are offended, you can keep quiet.

When an opportunity comes to honor God, you can seize it. The power is there.

Don't wait to feel it; just start using it. It's like sitting behind the wheel of a powerful car and wondering why you aren't going anywhere.

"This car doesn't go very fast. It's just sitting here!"

Try pressing down on that little pedal called the accelerator (and make sure your seatbelt is on).

We have all kinds of horsepower in the spiritual engine God has given us, yet we sit behind the wheel, waiting for a feeling or emotion, and wonder why we aren't going anywhere. We need to start living up to the name *Christian.*

YOUR FUTURE

God chose us. He saved us. He adopted us. He raised us from spiritual death. Why? Verse 7 of Ephesians 2 gives us the reason: "that in the ages to come He might show the exceeding riches of His grace in His kindness toward us in Christ Jesus."

He wants to show you how much He love you. He can't wait to reveal the glory He has waiting for you. And He is looking forward to your coming to Heaven.

Have you ever had a loved one who was away, and you couldn't wait for them to get home? Maybe you had done some remodeling on your house or had accomplished something wonderful. You couldn't wait for that person to get home so you could share it with him or her.

That is how God is. He can't wait for us to join Him in glory. In John 17, the true Lord's Prayer, Jesus said to the Father, "I want those you have given me to be with me where I am, and to see my glory, the glory you have given me because you loved me before the creation of the world" (verse 24 NIV).

Have you ever been to an unbelievable vacation spot or had an amazing meal at a certain restaurant? You don't keep it to yourself, do you? You tell other people about that place because you want them to enjoy it, too. That is how God feels about Heaven. No wonder David said of God, "In Your presence is fullness of joy; at Your right hand are pleasures forevermore" (Psalm 16:11).

The apostle Paul had the unique experience of dying and going to Heaven, probably after an angry crowd had stoned him. He wrote, "I was caught up to paradise and heard things so astounding that they cannot be expressed in words, things no human is allowed to tell" (2 Corinthians 12:4 NLT). From that moment on, Paul was homesick for Heaven. He said, "For to me, living means living for Christ, and dying is even better. But if I live, I can do more fruitful work for Christ. So I really don't know which is better. I'm torn between two desires: I long to go and be with Christ, which would be far better for me" (Philippians 1:21–23 NLT). *Far better* could be translated "much, much better." Or, as they would say in Hawaii, "Mo betta, brah."

Paul was saying, "Heaven would be much, much better. I'm homesick."

In the original language, when Paul spoke of departing to be with Christ, it carried the meaning of breaking camp, or literally, "to strike the tent." That is my favorite part of camping, because I know I'm going to have a hot shower and a warm meal very soon.

Your body is a tent, a temporary dwelling. It is not meant to last forever. And one day you will move from a tent to a mansion.

Paul recognized that. That was his hope. Is it yours as well?

You can know by saying yes to Jesus and asking Him to forgive you. Then you can have absolute certainty that when you leave Earth, you will go to Heaven.

5

PREPARED FOR GOOD WORKS

For we are His workmanship, created in Christ Jesus for good works, which God prepared beforehand that we should walk in them.(Ephesians 2:10)

Have you ever heard the French expression *pièce de résistance*? It's used to describe the best of something. If you're preparing a meal, it is the main event. It is the ultimate, the masterpiece.

Did you know that God has a *pièce de résistance*? Would it be the Alps, as amazing as they are? Maybe it is the islands of Hawaii or Tahiti. Or how about the solar system? As incredible as all of those things are, they are not God's masterpieces.

I want to tell you who God's masterpiece is right now. It is *me* . . . and it is *you*, too. We are God's masterpiece. We are His crowning achievement in creation. That is what we discover as we look at the second chapter of Ephesians.

We read in Ephesians 2:10 that "we are His workmanship, created in Christ Jesus for good works." *Workmanship* comes from the Greek word *poiema*, from which we get our English word *poem*. This verse also could be translated, "We are God's work of art," or "We are His masterpiece."

Without question, mankind is God's greatest creation. We are not highly evolved animals, as some would say. We are uniquely made in the very image of God.

Let's stop for a moment and just think of the complexities of the human body. Start with the nose. Did you know the nose can recognize ten thousand different aromas? I think my wife can recognize twenty-five thousand. She has the most sensitive nose of any person I've met. She'll say, "Something doesn't smell right here," and then she'll take one bite and conclude it is rancid. Meanwhile, I've eaten all of it.

That brings us to the tongue. It has six thousand taste buds. In fact, I think I might have lost two hundred of them on the last pizza I ate because I couldn't wait until it cooled down.

Then there is the human brain, which contains ten billion nerve cells. Each nerve cell is connected to as many as ten thousand other nerve cells throughout the body, which contains enough blood vessels to circle the planet two and a half times.

God has created each of us with our own special DNA blueprint, contained within every single cell. It's been estimated that if a person's blueprint was written in a book, it would require two hundred thousand pages. That is just *your* blueprint. And God knows every word on every page.

One of God's most amazing gifts to us is memory. We have the capacity to store millions of bits of information, keep them in order, and recall them when needed. Scientists say that we never really forget anything; it's all stored in the databanks of our memories. According to some estimates, a brain can store one million billion bits of information in a lifetime.

David wrote in the Psalms, "You made all the delicate, inner parts of my body and knit me together in my mother's womb. Thank you for making me so wonderfully complex!

Your workmanship is marvelous—how well I know it"
(139:13–14 NLT).

David continues, "You watched me as I was being formed in utter seclusion, as I was woven together in the dark of the womb. You saw me before I was born. Every day of my life was recorded in your book. Every moment was laid out before a single day had passed" (verses 15–16 NLT).

By the way, I hope these verses lay to rest the idea that the Bible would allow for abortion. The Bible is very clear in pointing out that life begins at conception—not birth. And not only does life begin at conception, but God knows all about us, even before we were conceived. He has a plan for us that preceded our conception and birth.

God said to the prophet Jeremiah, "Before I formed you in the womb I knew you; before you were born I sanctified you; I ordained you a prophet to the nations" (Jeremiah 1:5).

In addition to being fearfully and wonderfully made, God has a custom-designed work He wants to do in and through us. Just as no two snowflakes are exactly alike, God has a unique plan for each of our lives. While certain things are true of all of us, there are unique things that God wants to do in and through each of us.

GOD'S MASTERPIECE

We are God's masterpiece, His *poiema*. Not only does this word speak of the most outstanding item in a creative artist's series of work, but it also speaks of something that is perfect.

When I look at myself, I don't see perfection. I don't see rhythm. I don't see orderliness. Instead, I see a mess. I see confusion. I see mistakes. But God looks at me—and He looks at you—as His masterpiece.

God also sees the end from the beginning. I simply see now and recognize that I have so far to go. But God sees what I am to become.

You may only see your flaws and imperfections. But God sees you for what you can be.

"You are My masterpiece," God says. "It will take a long time, but when I'm done, it will be amazing."

The Bible says that God "has made everything beautiful in its time" (Ecclesiastes 3:11). Things in life happen to us that, in the moment, are not beautiful. But one day God will make them beautiful . . . in His time.

Things happen to us in life that are not good. Yet, God promises, "All things work together for good to those who love God, to those who are the called according to His purpose." You have His Word on this.

God is not a doting Father who can't see His child's faults. Our Father in Heaven knows everything about us. He is omniscient, which means "all-knowing." He envisions what each of us will be, like an artist staring at a blank canvas. He is already thinking about the finished work.

I am a cartoonist. I especially like to do caricatures. A caricature exaggerates a person's features. When I do a caricature of guys and exaggerate a certain feature, like their ears, they usually laugh and see it as a joke. But I've learned over the years that women are more sensitive about this than men. When I draw women, I won't exaggerate anything. In fact, I try to make them look even better than they actually look, and they're still not happy!

Someone might peer over my shoulder when I'm drawing one of these caricatures and not see much of anything taking shape. But I see what I'm going to do. I already have the complete picture in my mind.

That is how God sees us. He sees what He will make us into.

A composer does this as well. He or she hears songs we would never hear. The story is told of Paul McCartney, who had a melody that kept going through his mind. He didn't have lyrics, so he called it "Scrambled Eggs." Then he figured it would be better if he replaced the words *scrambled eggs* with the word *yesterday*. It became the most recorded song in human history. (I think he still should record a version using *scrambled eggs*. It would be interesting.)

Poets have a way with words, knowing which ones to put together and which ones to leave out to create emotion. It's artistry.

God is the master artist, the ultimate composer, the greatest poet. And He has a plan for you because you are His *poiema*. You are His work of art.

We find an example of this in a man named Simon. Jesus gave him a new name: Peter, which means "rock." I think the other disciples must have been looking at each other and thinking, *Is Jesus joking? Rock? Do you know this guy Simon? He is impulsive. He is hot-headed. He is quick-tempered. You're calling him rock?*

Yes, that is exactly what Jesus called him. Jesus saw Peter for who he would become, not just for who he was.

When the angel called Gideon to deliver the Israelites from their enemies, the Midianites, Gideon was hiding, hoping they wouldn't see him. Then an angel appeared to him and said, "The lord is with you, you mighty man of valor!" (Judges 6:12).

The last thing Gideon looked like at that moment was a mighty man of valor. But God saw him for what he could become.

We look at ourselves and see a blank canvas. God sees a masterpiece. We see a lump of clay. God sees a beautiful sculpture. We see failure. God sees success. We see a Simon. God sees a Peter. We see a Gideon. God sees a mighty man of valor.

Like a master sculptor who is chipping away everything that is not needed, God is chipping away in your life. He is making you into what He has always wanted you to be.

You were marred by sin, but now God has chosen you. He has redeemed you. He has adopted you. He has sealed you into His family.

And as a new creation in Christ, as God's workmanship, you've been "created in Christ Jesus for good works, which God prepared beforehand that we should walk in them" (Ephesians 2:10).

You are a prepared person for a prepared work. Have you figured out what it is yet? A little time may have to pass before you can sort that out. Just know that you've been created for good works.

That brings us to a bedrock statement about the Christian faith. This is only true of the follower of Jesus Christ. It's something that every believer needs a working knowledge of. It's basic Christian doctrine. And if you miss this, you miss everything, because it tells us how and why we are Christians:

> For by grace you have been saved through
> faith, and that not of yourselves; it is the gift of
> God, not of works, lest anyone should boast.
> (Ephesians 2:8–9)

GRACE SAVES US

We are Christians entirely and solely because of the grace of God. Our salvation did not come through any human effort on our part. We did nothing to merit this. We did nothing to deserve this. It was grace.

What is grace? Let's compare it to a couple of other words: *justice* and *mercy*. Justice is getting what you deserve. Mercy is not getting what you deserve. And grace is getting what you don't deserve.

When someone has broken a law and committed a horrible crime, we demand justice. The offender is arrested, sent to court, and sentenced. He or she faced justice for the crime and got what was deserved.

Then again, there might be a time when you've hurt someone and asked for forgiveness. That person extended mercy and didn't give you what you deserved.

But grace is different. It's getting what we don't deserve.

Yet a lot of people misunderstand and think they are saved through human effort. They feel they are good enough to go to Heaven because they believe they are good. It's amazing that even in the church, some people will think, *I'm a good person, so I'm going to Heaven.*

As I've often said, Heaven is not a place for good people; it is a place for forgiven people.

There will be good people in hell, and there will be bad people in Heaven. Let me explain. By "good" people, I mean relatively good people who are still sinners. Being a good person or a moral person won't get you into Heaven.

On the other hand, there will be "bad" people in Heaven, because if a bad person will repent of his sin, Jesus Christ will extend His forgiveness—even in the last moments of someone's life.

"That isn't fair!" someone might say.

If we want fairness, then we'll need to go back to justice. We don't want justice. We don't want to get what we deserve. In fact, we don't even want mercy. We want grace. That is how we will get into Heaven. It will be because of God's grace.

I love this statement from Timothy Keller: "We are more sinful and flawed in ourselves than we ever dared believe, yet at the same time we are more loved and accepted in Jesus Christ than we ever dared hope."[1]

That is an excellent summation of what we have looked at in Ephesians 1 and 2 thus far.

God has had grace on you and me.

GRACE SUSTAINS US

Not only does God's grace save us, but it sustains us too.

The apostle Paul had some type of physical affliction that was severe enough to cause him to pray about it on multiple occasions. While we don't know exactly what it was, some commentators believe it may have been an injury he received during one of his multiple stonings. Remember, Paul was beaten with rods. He was adrift at sea. He was stoned. In all of that, surely he could have developed some kind of serious physical problem.

Whatever it was, he came to the Lord three times and asked Him to take it away. Paul called it a thorn in the flesh, a messenger of Satan sent to buffet him.

Here was God's response: "My *grace* is sufficient for you, for my power is made perfect in weakness" (2 Corinthians 12:9).

Sometimes God will take away your affliction, sometimes God will use your affliction to bring you to Him, and sometimes He will allow His affliction to stay because He will be glorified through it. He will be glorified despite your affliction. Your weakness will show others the power of God.

Maybe something has happened to you that doesn't make sense. God can be honored through that, because it is His grace that sustains us.

GRACE TRANSFORMS US

We are to extend to others the grace God has given us. God has shown us grace, so we had better show it to others.

Ephesians 4:29 tells us, "Don't use foul or abusive language. Let everything you say be good and helpful, so that your words will be an encouragement to those who hear them" (NLT). And we are told in Colossians 4:6 to "let [our] conversation be always full of grace" (NIV). We should extend grace and love to others. Yet some people are quick to judge. They are quick to believe the other person's motive is always impure or wrong. They are quick to criticize. I think it is better to have a lot of grace and acknowledge that we don't know all the facts.

The author of Hebrews warns, "Look after each other so that none of you fails to receive the grace of God. Watch out that no poisonous root of bitterness grows up to trouble you, corrupting many" (Hebrews 12:15 NLT). Why are many defiled when someone is bitter? Because bitter people can't keep it to themselves. They love to talk. They are always stirring it up, always spreading their resentment around.

We extend grace to others because God has given grace to us. But if we lose sight of that, we can end up becoming bitter people.

This brings us to the importance of having an effective testimony, which is the story of how we came to Christ. To me, the best kind of testimony is the one that gives the glory to God, not us. The best kind of testimony is also the one that never exaggerates the past. I've heard some people whose testimonies get more dramatic with each telling.

This is something we should never do as Christians. Tell the truth about who you were. Tell the truth about what God did for you. The real story is God's grace—not what you gave up to follow Christ. What you gave up was nothing compared to what God gave you in its place.

Take the apostle Paul, for example. He had a family pedigree that didn't stop. He was a religious leader, a member of the Jewish Sanhedrin. He was the man. But there came a point when Paul said, "But whatever were gains to me I now consider loss for the sake of Christ" (Philippians 3:7 NIV). Years ago, I was speaking at a church in Hawaii that held its services in a wild animal park. The animals roamed around, and the people in the church had become used to them. The morning I was speaking, a peacock walked into the service and strolled down the center aisle. He opened his tail feathers and slowly turned for his audience, which largely ignored him.

I, on the other hand, was distracted by our visitor. I had never had a peacock walk forward at an invitation before. He proceeded all the way down the aisle to the front of the stage, where he stopped and began making his peacock noises, which sounded a lot like a screaming girl. He did this again and again. Meanwhile, I was trying to speak. It was almost as though the peacock instinctively knew he was a magnificent creature.

A lot of Christians are like that peacock. They have an attitude that says, *I'm so spiritual now. I'm so godly. Just look at me!*

They love to talk about all they've given up to follow Jesus and the great sacrifices they've made. In reality, they gave up sin and misery and emptiness and a future in hell. And in exchange, God gave them purpose and forgiveness and the guaranteed hope of Heaven. That is the story we should tell when we talk to people about Jesus Christ.

The first sin ever committed was not on Earth but in Heaven. Do you know what it was? It was pride. Lucifer, a magnificent angelic being, wanted to take God's position. He said,

> "I will ascend to the heavens; I will raise my
> throne above the stars of God; I will sit enthroned
> on the mount of assembly, on the utmost heights
> of Mount Zaphon. I will ascend above the tops
> of the clouds; I will make myself like the Most
> High." (Isaiah 14:13–14 NIV)

As a result, God ejected Lucifer from that prominent position he once held in Heaven.

This should serve as a reminder not to look down on other people. You may look at people who aren't believers and think, *I'm so much better than they are.*

You are not *better* than they are; you are *better off* than they are. What has happened in your life is a result of the grace of God. You should look with compassion on those people. It is "not by works of righteousness which we have done, but according to His mercy He saved us" (Titus 3:5).

GROWING IN GRACE

We can never outgrow this grace, nor do we move beyond it. We need it for salvation. We need it to sustain us. We need it to transform us. And then we need to receive more of it throughout our lives.

We are told in Hebrews 4:16, "Let us then approach God's throne of grace with confidence, so that we may receive mercy and find grace to help us in our time of need" (NIV). I need God's grace. You need it, too. Therefore, we have no grounds for boasting.

How did you become a Christian? Was it because you were born into a Christian family? That may have helped to prepare your heart. But there still had to be a moment when you decided for yourself to follow Christ.

Are you a Christian because you have done a certain number of good deeds? No. If you find yourself boasting in anything you have done to obtain salvation, then either you are not a Christian, or you don't understand how to become one.

FAITH AND WORKS

There should be a balance between faith and works in our lives, however. Works don't save us, but they are good evidence that we are saved. Good works do not precede conversion, but they should always follow it.

Just as it is a great mistake to think your salvation comes by works, it is also a mistake to think your salvation should not produce any works or results. James says, "But someone will say, 'You have faith, and I have works.' Show me your faith without your works, and I will show you my faith by my works.

You believe that there is one God. You do well. Even the demons believe—and tremble! But do you want to know, O foolish man, that faith without works is dead?" (2:18–20).

Nonbelievers cannot see your faith, but they can see your works. (That is all they can see.) If you were arrested for being a Christian, would there be enough evidence to convict you? If they interviewed your husband or wife and asked, "What is this person really like in the home? Is this really a man of God? Is this really a woman of God?" what would they find out?

If they asked your kids, "Are your parents godly examples?" or asked your coworkers, "Does this person work hard? Are they diligent? Are they honest?" would there be evidence?

People can tell when someone is a Christian by the way he or she lives. A Christian should want to bring glory to God.

Some people have good works, but they don't have God. I have met non-Christians whom I think are fine, upstanding people. Their good works, however, won't get them into Heaven. It is only faith in Jesus Christ that will.

You may say, "I don't believe in works; I'm going to Heaven because of the grace of God."

Okay. But my question for you is what have you done for God lately? You may criticize someone who goes out and does good things because they think by doing them, they will get to Heaven. But at the same time, you're doing nothing.

You should not do good works to earn God's approval. You already have God's approval. But because you have it, should it not produce results in your life? And if it doesn't produce good works, are you really a Christian? Do you really understand what the grace of God is?

The Bible tells us many times to produce good works. Jesus said, "Let your light shine before others, that they may see your good deeds and glorify your Father in heaven" (Matthew 5:16 NIV).

Paul tells us, "God is able to bless you abundantly, so that in all things at all times, having all that you need, you will abound in every good work," and he encourages us to "live a life worthy of the Lord and please him in every way: bearing fruit in every good work, growing in the knowledge of God" (2 Corinthians 9:8; Colossians 1:10 NIV).

You can't have one without the other, as James pointed out. It's sort of like two wings of an airplane. You need both to fly. If one wing is missing, that plane will not stay aloft. And if you have a lopsided Christian who has only faith but not works, that Christian is missing it. If you have a person who only has works but doesn't have faith, then they too are missing it. It is like inhaling and exhaling. Faith is taking the gospel in; works is taking the gospel out.

Sometimes people will set up a false dichotomy between the writings of Paul and James. Yet both are inspired by God. Paul, the so-called advocate of faith, speaks of being rich in good works. And James, the so-called exponent of works, said we should be rich in faith. We need both in our lives. But let's get them in the right order. First there is the faith. Then the works come as a result.

PREPARED FOR A PURPOSE

God is preparing the way for you in life. He is manipulating all the resources of the universe so the work He wants to do in your life will be completed. That includes setbacks and even crises.

We see this in the story of Joseph, who suffered horrible mistreatment at the hands of his jealous brothers. They sold him into slavery, thinking they would never see him again. But because God had His hand on Joseph, this young man was elevated to become the second-most powerful man in Egypt, second only to the Pharaoh. He was in charge of Egypt's food supply because he correctly interpreted the Pharaoh's dreams.

When his brothers arrived in Egypt, Joseph could have had them all executed on the spot. No one would have questioned his decision. Instead, Joseph said to his brothers, "You intended to harm me, but God intended it all for good. He brought me to this position so I could save the lives of many people" (Genesis 50:20 NLT).

Amazing. I wonder if it dawned on Joseph at that very moment. I wonder if he suddenly realized that his exile, with all the brutality, pain, sorrow, rejection, and false accusations, not only had been allowed by God, but had been mightily used by Him to prepare Joseph to do so much for others.

In the same way, God is preparing you for a purpose. When things seem to be randomly happening in your life, remember that God is never caught by surprise. You will never hear the Lord say, "Wait . . . what?"

God knows exactly what is going on. Either He allows it, or He is doing it.

Let God have His loving way with you. Yield to the molding of His hand and the strokes of His brush. He is trying to help you fulfill your reason for existence. He is putting His finishing touches on you as His masterpiece.

By grace you have been saved through faith . . . not of works, lest anyone should boast.

God extends the grace. You apply the faith.

6

YOUR ALL-ACCESS PASS

For Christ himself has brought peace to us. He united Jews and Gentiles into one people when, in his own body on the cross, he broke down the wall of hostility that separated us.(Ephesians 2:14 NIV)

It has been said that men can live forty days without food, three days without water, eight minutes without air, but not one second without hope.

In what are you putting your hope today? A political party? Technology? Personal possessions?

None of these will help us in our hour of need. There is only one whom we can legitimately put our hope in, and that is God Himself.

The apostle Paul summed this up perfectly for us when he wrote of life apart from Christ:

> Remember that at that time you were separate from Christ, excluded from citizenship in Israel and foreigners to the covenants of the promise, without hope and without God in the world. (Ephesians 2:12 niv)

That is your story. That is my story. There was a time in our lives when we were without God. And because of that, we were without hope. When there is no God, there is no hope. But when you know God, you have great hope. This has come about because of what Jesus did on the cross.

One of the most significant events of the twentieth century was the fall of the Berlin Wall. After World War II, a wall was erected to keep people in East Berlin and other influences out. (In the United States, we put up walls to keep people out. But in communist countries, they put up walls to keep people in.)

Many people tried to get over the Berlin Wall through the years to escape the horrible oppression they lived under. Eighty people died in their attempts to get over that wall. Only a handful succeeded.

President Reagan went to that wall in 1987, and at a public gathering, he openly addressed Mikhail Gorbachev, the leader of Russia at the time, and spoke these famous words: "Mr. Gorbachev, tear down this wall!"

Gorbachev never did tear down that wall. But the people of East Germany finally did. In 1989, world history was made as the border opened. Ultimately the wall was destroyed and freedom was restored.

A wall far more formidable than the Berlin Wall has been torn down. It's the wall that kept all of us separated from God: the wall of sin. Two thousand years ago, Jesus tore down that wall, giving us free, open, and constant access into His presence. This was done because His blood was shed for us. Notice verse 14 of Ephesians 2: "For Christ himself has brought peace to us. He united Jews and Gentiles into one people when, in his own body on the cross, he broke down the wall of hostility that separated us" (NLT).

WHAT THE DEVIL DOESN'T WANT YOU TO KNOW

I'm about to tell you something the Devil doesn't want you to know. Read carefully, because this could affect your Christian life. The Devil would like you to believe the way to approach God is on the basis of your good works, as though you were still living under the law.

If you were a Jew living under the old covenant, you would approach God through the high priest, who would symbolically place your sins on the animal that would be slain for you. Through your works and efforts, you would hope that you could have a relationship with God.

Sometimes as Christians, we still think that way. We'll look at our lives and begin to reason, *I read the Bible every morning— and I even read an extra chapter on Wednesday. I shared the gospel with a couple of people, too. I remembered to pray. I went to a midweek Bible study. I feel like my life is so right with God that I can approach Him now.*

Then maybe we don't do as well the next week. We sleep in. We don't tell anyone about Jesus. In fact, we yell at a few drivers on the freeway. And we don't make it to the midweek Bible study. As a result, we think, *I can't approach God. I'm not worthy.*

Christians who think that way are in a works-righteousness relationship with God. As I pointed out earlier, there is a place for works, but there also is a place for evidence and results in our lives as followers of Jesus. We need to understand that as followers of Christ, our access to God is not based on what we do but on what Jesus has done for us.

God's love for us is not dependent on your progress; it is based on His perfection.

The law of God demands that we do it all; God's grace reminds us that He paid it all.

The law demands everything and gives nothing; God's grace gives everything and demands nothing.

The Devil doesn't want you to know that. He wants you to think you can't approach God when you have sinned. But that is *the time* to approach God. And you come to Him through the shed blood of Jesus Christ.

Sometimes I think we underestimate how messed up we really were before we became Christians. We underestimate what drastic measures God took to reach us and change our eternal address. We were worse off than we ever thought we were. That is the bad news. The good news is that we are more loved than we ever thought possible.

It has been said that you can tell the depth of a well by how much rope you have to lower to reach the bottom. God had to lower a lot of rope, so to speak, to reach us in our sinful state. That is demonstrated in the death of Jesus.

Sometimes we think we can draw near to God because we feel really good about it. At other times we think we cannot draw near to God because we don't feel really good about it. Our emotions can mislead us. They can get the best of us.

"I just listen to my heart," some people say.

Be careful. Our hearts can mislead us. Our hearts can condemn us. In fact, the Bible reminds us, "For if our heart condemns us, God is greater than our heart, and knows all things" (1 John 3:20).

Whatever you have done, you can approach God because Jesus' blood was shed. Hebrews 10:19–22 tells us,

We can boldly enter heaven's Most Holy Place because of the blood of Jesus. By his death, Jesus opened a new and life-giving way through the curtain into the Most Holy Place. And since we have a great High Priest who rules over God's house, let us go right into the presence of God with sincere hearts fully trusting him. For our guilty consciences have been sprinkled with Christ's blood to make us clean, and our bodies have been washed with pure water. (NLT)

In the book of Revelation, we read about Satan being cast down, along with his angels. The passage goes on to say,

Then I heard a loud voice saying in heaven, "Now salvation, and strength, and the kingdom of our God, and the power of His Christ have come, for the accuser of our brethren, who accused them before our God day and night, has been cast down. And they overcame him by the blood of the Lamb and by the word of their testimony, and they did not love their lives to the death." (12:10–11)

If you want to overcome Satan, then you need to start working out how the blood of the Lamb, Jesus Christ, operates in your life. You can approach God because Jesus opened the way for you. You can ask for His forgiveness. Of course, Satan doesn't want you to know that. He would like you to think that you can only approach God if you are worthy.

RECOGNIZE THE DIFFERENCE

We need to draw a distinction between Satan's accusations and the Spirit's conviction. When the Holy Spirit of God convicts you, He uses the Word of God in love to bring you back into fellowship with God the Father. In contrast, when Satan accuses you, he will use your own sins in a hateful way to destroy you. He wants you to feel helpless and hopeless.

That is what happened to Judas Iscariot. He listened to the Devil, and he went out and hung himself after his betrayal of Christ. Jesus would have forgiven Judas if he had repented. In the Garden of Gethsemane, Judas had to identify Jesus with a kiss. As he approached Him, Jesus said, "Friend, why have you come?" (Matthew 26:50).

Jesus knew what Judas was doing. In fact, He already had identified him in the Upper Room and told Judas, "What you do, do quickly" (John 13:27). In that moment, Jesus was offering to Judas one last chance to repent. But Judas didn't listen to Jesus. He listened to Satan, and he hung himself.

Simon Peter also betrayed the Lord. He openly denied Him three times and claimed he never knew Jesus. Then he went out and wept bitterly. But he returned to Christ because he listened to the Holy Spirit.

Let me sum it up this way: Satan will always drive you *from* the Cross; the Holy Spirit will always lead you *to* the Cross.

Satan wants you to think that it is all based on your worthiness and your works.

You can approach God whenever you want because of the open access that Jesus Himself provides. Let's understand how this works in our lives and start applying it.

When we mess up and sin, here is what we need to know: we can approach God.

The Devil, however, will say, "No, you can't approach God."

Yes, we can.

The Devil will say, "Don't pray. Don't read your Bible. Don't go to church."

Don't listen to him. The Holy Spirit will convict you to bring you to the solution you need—not to condemn you. The Holy Spirit will show you your sin to bring you to Jesus, who will forgive you and restore your fellowship with Him—not to drive you away in despair.

APPLY THE BLOOD

When we have sinned and feel like we can't approach God, when our emotions are telling us that we never can pray again, we need to say, "I can approach God right now because of the blood of Jesus Christ."

When God brought a series of plagues on Egypt and was about to kill all the firstborn in the land in the tenth and final plague, He first gave a command to His people, the Jews:

> "Go, pick out a lamb or young goat for each of your families, and slaughter the Passover animal. Drain the blood into a basin. Then take a bundle of hyssop branches and dip it into the blood. Brush the hyssop across the top and sides of the doorframes of your houses. And no one may go out through the door until morning. For the Lord will pass through the land to strike down the Egyptians. But when he sees the blood on the top and sides of the doorframe, the Lord will pass over your home." (Exodus 12:21–23 NLT)

That is what they did. (By the way, the blood on the top, right, and left doorframe looks like a cross.) As the judgment of God came, He passed over every home that had the blood on the doorframe.

A Jew who heard that command but decided not to apply the blood on his home would have faced that judgment. But, of course, they obeyed God, and they were spared from judgment.

It is the same in our lives as well. We apply the shed blood of Jesus Christ.

Ephesians assures us, "But now you have been united with Christ Jesus. Once you were far away from God, but now you have been brought near to him through the blood of Christ" (2:13 NLT).

When we have sinned, we can go to God at any time and ask for His forgiveness. In 1 John 1:9 we read, "If we confess our sins, He is faithful and just to forgive us our sins and to cleanse us from all unrighteousness."

Know this: if you have unconfessed sin in your life, it effectively will bring your prayer life to a halt. The psalmist wrote, "If I had cherished sin in my heart, the Lord would not have listened" (Psalm 66:18 NIV). And Isaiah 59:1–2 says, "The Lord's arm is not too weak to save you, nor is his ear too deaf to hear you call. It's your sins that have cut you off from God. Because of your sins, he has turned away and will not listen anymore" (NLT). We have to come to God, admit our sin, turn from it, and apply the blood of Jesus in our lives—the blood of Jesus shed for us.

We can know, regardless of how we feel afterward, that we are restored to God.

Even after you've prayed, you might say, "I still don't feel it."

Don't worry about what you *feel*. This is based on what God has done for you.

Just consider these amazing contrasts in Ephesians:

> We were without Christ (2:12); we are in Christ (2:13).

> We were strangers (2:12); we are no longer strangers (2:19).

> We had no hope (2:12); we are called in one hope (4:4).

> We were without God (2:12); God is our Father (1:2–3)

> We were far off (2:13); we have been brought near by the blood of Christ (2:13).

BE RECONCILED TO GOD

Because the blood of Jesus was shed, we can come into a relationship with Christ. We can be reconciled to God.

We also can be reconciled to one another. Ephesians 2 continues,

> For Christ himself has brought peace to us. He united Jews and Gentiles into one people when, in his own body on the cross, he broke down the wall of hostility that separated us. He did this by ending the system of law with its commandments

and regulations. He made peace between Jews and Gentiles by creating in himself one new people from the two groups. Together as one body, Christ reconciled both groups to God by means of his death on the cross, and our hostility toward each other was put to death. (verses 14–16 NLT)

The word *reconcile* means "to bring together again."

There is a lot of talk today about reconciliation, from racial and cultural reconciliation to generational reconciliation. These are valid concerns. But any attempt to bridge a generation gap or a racial or cultural divide that doesn't include Christ is doomed to failure.

We can talk all day long about getting people together, but just come to church and watch what God does. When we don't make it about our differences and instead pull together for what we hold in common, suddenly those differences begin to melt away. First we are reconciled to God. Then we can be reconciled to one another.

The apostle Paul put it this way: "There is neither Jew nor Gentile, neither slave nor free, nor is there male and female, for you are all one in Christ Jesus. If you belong to Christ, then you are Abraham's seed, and heirs according to the promise" (Galatians 3:28–29 NIV). Sin is the great separator of the world. It has been dividing people since the very beginning of human history.

When Adam and Eve sinned, they were separated from God. Then their children Cain and Abel were born. Cain murdered his brother Abel, and it went from bad to worse.

As Genesis progresses, it gets so bad that violence fills the world. God says He will judge Earth with a flood, and He directs a man named Noah to build an ark. Noah, his family, and the animals placed there are protected in the ark when the flood comes. They eventually come to dry land and a new earth God has blessed them with.

You would have thought that everything would be great after that. The problem was they still had sinful hearts.

It wasn't long until men began building a tower to the heavens called Babel. Effectively, it was the first attempt by human beings to establish religion. God brought another judgment, separating the people by dividing their languages.

Then God raised up Abraham and set him apart. From Abraham came the Jewish people, who were in a special covenant with God—and they still are. God still has a plan for the Jewish people. He still has a plan for the nation of Israel. God set them apart. And it was from the Jewish people that our Messiah, Jesus, came.

Jesus went to the cross and died there for us, opening up access to God.

Years ago when we were holding one of our crusades out of state, I arrived at the crusade and realized I had forgotten my Bible at the hotel. I asked my son Christopher to go back to the hotel room and get my Bible. He rushed back to the hotel and retrieved my Bible.

But as he made his way back to where I was in the stadium, an usher stopped him and said, "You can't come in here."

Christopher said, "I need to get in there. I'm taking this Bible to my dad, Greg Laurie."

"How do I know your dad is Greg Laurie?" he said. "You don't have the proper pass."

So Christopher pulled out his driver's license. "Look, my name is Christopher David Laurie. This is my dad. Look, his name is on the Bible! I'm taking the Bible to my dad!"

He still didn't believe Christopher, so finally I spoke with the man on the phone and told him, "He is my son. Let him in, please—and do it quickly if you wouldn't mind."

It was through our relationship that Christopher could get through.

In the same way, we can approach God through relationship. It is not because we earned it. We once were far away and "have been brought near by the blood of Christ" (Ephesians 2:13 NIV).

We never get past this. This is the A to Z of the gospel. We start with the gospel and end with the gospel.

We never move on from this because we still sin, and we need to come back to God again and again.

Everything has changed because of the blood of Jesus. It is not about what we do; it is about what He has done.

Because of His shed blood, we can come to Him. We have an all-access pass.

7

AT HOME IN YOUR HEART

Then Christ will make his home in your hearts as you trust in
him. Your roots will grow down into God's love and keep you
strong.(Ephesians 3:17 NLT)

A mother was telling her little daughter that Jesus lived in her
heart, so the little girl put her ear to her mom's chest.
  "What are you doing?" the mother asked.

  "I'm listening for Jesus."

  "What is He saying right now?"

  The little girl listened a little more. Then she said, "Right
now, I think He's making coffee."

  Perhaps you've heard the expressions "receive Jesus Christ
into your life" or "ask Jesus to come into your heart." Is it actually biblical to say such a thing?

  Yes, it is.

  Colossians 1:27 says, "And this is the secret: Christ lives
in you" (NLT). Then we are told in John 1:12, "But as many as
received Him, to them He gave the right to become children of
God" (emphasis added).

Jesus said in John 14:23, "All who love me will do what I say. My Father will love them, and we will come and make our home with each of them" (NLT). Therefore, Christ does come to live inside of us. Indeed, we do receive Him. God does make His home with us.

But when it comes to this topic, perhaps the most oft-quoted verse is Revelation 3:20, where Jesus says, "Behold, I stand at the door and knock. If anyone hears My voice and opens the door, I will come in to him and dine with him, and he with Me."

Contextually, that statement was given to the church of Laodicea, which Jesus described as a lukewarm church. (In fact, I think the question could be raised as to whether many of the people in this church even were believers.)

To the compromised person, the lukewarm person, the person who is not as committed as her or she ought to be, Jesus is saying, "I stand at the door and knock. If anyone hears My voice and opens the door, I will come in to him and dine with him, and he with Me."

The meaning of Jesus dining with us is lost on our fast-food culture. The idea of dining is lost on us in many ways in the twenty-first century. But in the first century, in the days of Jesus, they didn't have drive-through restaurants. They didn't have a McDavid's or a Falafel Bell.

There were no televisions, computer games, tablet devices, or iPhones. At the end of the day, you would sit down to a long, leisurely meal and relax with family and your close friends. It was a time to let your hair down (in my case, that is singular). The idea was to enjoy fellowship one with another. The meal was the main event of the day.

So when Jesus says, "If anyone hears My voice and opens the door, I will come in to him and dine with him," that is the idea. Jesus is saying, "We'll spend time together."

Have you ever had someone you didn't know that well invite you to dinner? You are kind of reluctant. You think, *Dinner is long. That's a lot of time with someone I don't know very well.* You aren't sure you want to have dinner with them, especially if they're trying to sell you something.

Or, if someone comes over to your house whom you don't know very well, you might bring them into your living room or perhaps your family room.

But if a friend or family comes over, where do they go? Into your kitchen. What is it with kitchens? I've noticed that no matter how big or beautiful the home, everyone ends up in the kitchen. It's where the food is prepared, where the action is. There's just something about it. If you are especially close to someone, you may even let them raid your fridge or take a little food off your plate.

That is the idea when Jesus says He wants to dine with us.

Do you think Jesus is comfortable hanging out with you? Are you the kind of person that He could have a long, leisurely meal with? Could He actually raid your fridge or take some food off your plate if He wanted to? Is that the kind of relationship you have? Or, is it more formal or a bit removed?

Before you answer that question, let's briefly reflect on what we've learned so far.

"WHEN I THINK OF ALL THIS . . ."

At the beginning of Ephesians 3, Paul goes over some of his older material, so to speak. He writes,

> When I think of all this, I, Paul, a prisoner of
> Christ Jesus for the benefit of you Gentiles . . .

assuming, by the way, that you know God gave me the special responsibility of extending his grace to you Gentiles. As I briefly wrote earlier, God himself revealed his mysterious plan to me. (verses 1–3 NLT)

Paul draws on what he has already said in this epistle. Thus, here are four truths to remember so far.

The person who puts his or her faith in Christ becomes altogether new. Paul tells us in Ephesians 2:14–15, "For he himself is our peace, who has made the two groups one and has destroyed the barrier, the dividing wall of hostility, by setting aside in his flesh the law with its commands and regulations. His purpose was to create in himself one new humanity out of the two, thus making peace" (NIV).

All believers, Jews and Gentiles, are now one body. This may not seem like a big deal to us today, but it was a revolutionary thought in the first century. There was no relationship between Gentiles and Jews. But now, because of Christ, the wall of separation has been broken down.

We who were far away from God have been brought near by the blood of Christ. We were away from God. But because the blood of Jesus was shed on the cross, we can approach God at any time (see Ephesians 2:13). It is not based on our worthiness or merit. It is because He shed His blood for us.

All believers are equal citizens of God's kingdom and family. One person is not better than another. In verse 19 of Ephesians 2 we read, "So now you Gentiles are no longer strangers and foreigners. You are citizens along with all of God's holy people. You are members of God's family."

PAUL THE PRISONER

Notice from Ephesians 3:1 that Paul is writing these words as a prisoner: "When I think of all this, I, Paul, a prisoner of Christ Jesus . . ." Most commentators believe Paul wrote this when he was incarcerated in Rome. I find it interesting, however, that Paul describes himself not as a prisoner of Rome but as a prisoner of Christ.

It's as though Paul was saying, "I understand that even though I am in a place I don't want to be, God has allowed it."

Paul recognized he had been placed there by God. It was Paul who wrote Romans 8:28 after all: "And we know that all things work together for good to those who love God, to those who are the called according to His purpose." Paul saw God's bigger picture.

Sometimes we get angry when we're in a place we don't want to be. Maybe it's in a hospital bed as a result of an accident, or maybe it's in a conflict that someone else created. Did you ever stop and think that God allowed it for a purpose? If you are His child, then you had better start thinking about it.

Paul said something similar in Ephesians 3:13: "So please don't lose heart because of my trials here. I am suffering for you, so you should feel honored" (NLT). Paul acknowledged he was a prisoner because of his preaching, and he was suffering for the Gentiles.

I have something to say to those who feel called to be a leader in the church some day. There is a cost to being a leader. In fact, leaders sometimes suffer for others. Paul wrote in 2 Corinthians 1:6, "Even when we are weighed down with troubles, it is for your comfort and salvation! For when we ourselves are comforted, we will certainly comfort you. Then you can patiently endure the same things we suffer" (NLT). Why do leaders suffer? Sometimes it's so they can offer help to others who are suffering.

The most devastating day in our lives was on July 24, 2008. Our oldest son, Christopher, who was working at our church as the lead designer, died in an automobile accident.

Our hearts are still broken, and we miss him each and every day.

In the aftermath of this horrific tragedy, people would ask me, "Why did God allow this to happen to *you*?" Think the implication was that preachers get a free pass on pain, that we don't have to go through the same trials and hardships as other human beings.

But that isn't true. Leaders suffer as every person suffers. The difference might be that we have a platform we can use to help others.

I never really desired a ministry to those who had lost loved ones, especially children, but I have one now. I have joined a very exclusive "club" I never wanted to be a member of.

I feel I can speak for parents who have lost children and to them.

Hardly a day goes by when I don't hear of someone reaching out to me because the "worst-case scenario" has happened to them—the death of a child.

I try to do what I can to bring comfort and hope to them.

That is what Paul was saying. He went through these things so he could comfort others with the comfort he received from God.

I wish we didn't have to go through bad things. I wish we didn't have to face challenges and hardships. God allows it for His purposes, and one day we will know why. In the interim, let's not waste our pain. Let's not indulge in a pity party. Instead let's leverage it for God's glory and use it as a tool to help other people.

I'm not saying that we go through bad things just so we can help others. But what I am saying is that we do go through bad things, period. So let's help others.

A HEAVENLY AUDIENCE

In verse 10, Paul shifts gears to an interesting little portion of Ephesians 3:

> "To the intent that now the manifold wisdom of God might be made known by the church to the principalities and powers in the heavenly places."

Did you know that angels are watching you right now?

"Does that mean we have guardian angels?" you might ask.

I don't know. Probably. We have angels around us. Psalm 34:7 says, "The angel of the Lord encamps all around those who fear Him, and delivers them."

Not only are angels watching over us, but angels are learning from us. It doesn't seem possible that these magnificent spirit beings, who have seen so many things in the presence of God that we've never seen, could actually learn from us.

But look again at verse 10 of Ephesians 3: "To the intent that now the manifold wisdom of God might be made known *by the church* to the principalities and powers in the heavenly places" (emphasis added). Underline that phrase *by the church*. God will show His wisdom by the church, or through the church, to whom? To the principalities and powers in the heavenly places. That is referring to angelic beings.

According to the Greek scholar Kenneth Wuest, the word *by* comes from a Greek proposition that speaks of immediate agency. In other words, it is by the church these truths are known.

Angels have seen some amazing things. They have contemplated the glory of God for all these years. But they learn something from the church that only we can teach them, because in the church they see what God did for us to reach us.

They saw the incarnation of our Lord when He came to Earth as a helpless little baby, born in the manger in Bethlehem. They saw the sacrifice of Christ on the cross of Calvary for humanity. They see what happens when God transforms a human life and the difference it makes. It blows their minds.

In fact, we are told in 1 Peter 1:12, "And now this Good News has been announced to you by those who preached in the power of the Holy Spirit sent from heaven. It is all so wonderful that even the angels are eagerly watching these things happen" (NLT). Another way to translate it is, "The angels are bending low and looking into this."

It's as though the angels are saying, "Look at this. Look at what God is doing with these people. This is amazing!"

Yes, angels are watching, and they're learning from us.

PAUL'S PRAYER

Paul has dealt at great length with our privileges and spiritual riches we have in Christ. Now he prays a prayer for the power we need to put them into use:

For this reason I bow my knees to the Father of our Lord Jesus Christ, from whom the whole family in heaven and earth is named, that He would grant you, according to the riches of His glory, to be strengthened with might through His Spirit in the inner man, that Christ may dwell in your hearts through faith; that you, being rooted and grounded in love, may be able to comprehend with all the saints what *is* the width and length and depth and height—to know the love of Christ which passes knowledge; that you may be filled with all the fullness of God. (Ephesians 3:14–19)

This is the second of two prayers recorded in Ephesians. The first is in Ephesians 1:18–19, where the emphasis is on enlightenment.

Now, in this prayer in Ephesians 3, the emphasis is on empowerment. Paul was saying, in effect, "I want you to know how much is there. Now, I want you to unleash it."

Imagine how mind-blowing it would be to go to the bank with your ATM card, and when you check your balance, you discover you have $10 million in your account.

Paul was saying, "I pray that you will see what God has put into your spiritual bank account."

Then Paul talks about the width, depth, and height of God's love. He wasn't saying there are four kinds of love. He simply was saying that no matter where you look, there is God's love. You look up, and there is God's love. You look down . . . to the right . . . to the left—God's love is there, as far as you can see.

If you want to see the length of God's love, you will find it in how He chose us before the foundation of the world (see Ephesians 1:4–5).

You can see the breath of God's love in that He chose both Gentiles and Jews and brought us all into the family of God (see Ephesians 2:11–18).

Next, you can see the height of God's love in blessing us with every spiritual blessing in the heavenly places (see Ephesians 1:3).

And then you can see the depth of God's love in reaching down to us in our sinful state (see Ephesians 2:1–5).

What Paul prays next is interesting: "that Christ may dwell in your hearts through faith" (3:17). Paul is saying, "My prayer for you is that Christ would dwell in your hearts." Who is he writing to here? Is Paul addressing nonbelievers?

No, these are the believers in Ephesus. We've already discovered they have been called, redeemed, adopted, justified, and sealed by the Holy Spirit. Why would Paul ask for Christ to dwell in a heart like that?

For the answer to that question, we have to go back to the original language. The word Paul used here for *dwell* is a compound Greek word that basically means "to live in a house." But when a prefix is added, the word comes to mean "to settle down, to be at home in a house."

Paul isn't simply saying, "My prayer is that Christ would come and live in your heart." Rather, Paul was saying, "I'm praying that He will come settle down and be comfortable in your heart and life."

It isn't that we just give Jesus a place. *Lord, here is your spot, this little closet. That is yours. You can live there and come out on Sundays, and we will talk a little at that time. Then I will put you back into the closet. The rest of this house is mine. You are my honored guest, Lord.*

Jesus doesn't want to be your honored guest; He wants to be a permanent resident. He wants the title deed. He wants the master key. He is Master. He is Lord. He is the boss man—not the honored guest. That is what Paul is saying.

Do you think that is a description of your heart right now? Coming back to my earlier question, do you think Jesus is comfortable hanging out with you?

We find an example of this in Genesis, in the lives of Abraham and Lot. Although these two men happen to be related, we see a fascinating contrast between their lives. On one hand, Abraham walked with God. On the other hand, Lot walked with his uncle Abraham.

There are men and women who are very godly and have their own relationship with the Lord. Then there are other people who will hang around people like that for a time and will be doing pretty well. But the moment they are away from the influence of godly people, they immediately are dragged down. Instead of being a godly influence somewhere else, they are the ones who are influenced. Which category are you in? Are you an influencer? Or, are you easily influenced by others?

Abraham walked with God, but Lot's life was not of that caliber. One day, three angels came to visit Abraham. Many Bible commentators believe that one of those angels was Christ Himself. It may have been a Christophany, an appearance of Christ in the Old Testament.

These visitors come to Abraham, the man of God, who is in the middle of God's will, doing God's work in God's way. He lived in Mamre, which means "fatness" or "well-fed." You could say that Abraham was spiritually fat and sassy. He was doing well. He was close to God. Then along came these three heavenly messengers, possibly two angels and the Lord Himself. They spent time with Abraham.

In contrast, Lot was living in Sodom, a city known for excessive wickedness and depravity. Lot was in an ungodly place with ungodly people tolerating ungodly things.

Christ came to both Abraham and Lot in effect—or at least the angels did. They were in different positions at the time. Abraham was sitting at the entrance of his tent (see Genesis 18:1), while Lot was sitting in the gateway of the city (see Genesis 19:1). Abraham lived in tents, and the Bible tells us that "he was looking forward to the city with foundations, whose architect and builder is God" (Hebrews 11:10 NIV). Abraham knew that his ultimate home was Heaven.

On more than one occasion, the Bible calls our bodies *tents*. Tents aren't meant to last forever. You can stretch them all you want and do whatever you want to your tent, but it will wear out eventually. Our bodies are temporary, but one day as Christians, we will receive glorified, radically upgraded versions. One day we will be in a sinless state. One day we will be in Heaven. We know as we walk through life on Earth that we are sojourners. We are pilgrims. We are visitors. Our eternal home is in Heaven.

That doesn't mean we are disconnected from the world we live in. I think Christians can enjoy life more than anyone. We know the God who made it. I find that those who think the most about the next life have the best version of this life. I think C. S. Lewis said it best in *Mere Christianity*: "Aim at Heaven and you get earth 'thrown in': aim at earth and you get neither."[1]

Abraham understood this, but Lot didn't. When the three heavenly visitors arrived, Abraham was sitting at the entrance of his tent. He invited his guests to a meal and whipped up a feast for them, and Abraham and his visitors had a nice, long time of fellowship.

On the other hand, they found Lot sitting at the entrance to Sodom, which indicated he was a leader there. Lot invited them to his house, but they said, "No . . . we will spend the night in the open square" (Genesis 19:2).

Talk about rejection. Can you imagine? The angels were essentially saying, "No, we would rather stand in the street."

Finally Lot convinced them to come inside. And as they were having a meal together, the citizens of Sodom started banging on the door because they saw these strange visitors.

They said, "Where are the men who came to you tonight? Bring them out to us that we may know them carnally" (verse 5). In other words, "Send these men out to us so we may have sex with them." That is how twisted this culture was.

Lot, showing how compromised he was, said to them, "No, my friends. Don't do this wicked thing. Look, I have two daughters who have never slept with a man. Let me bring them out to you, and you can do what you like with them" (Genesis 19:7–8 NIV). How would you like to have been one of Lot's daughters? What kind of father does that? Lot was upside down. And if you only read the Genesis account of Lot, you might think he wasn't a believer—in the Old Testament context.

But he was. In the New Testament, he is referred to as "righteous Lot" (2 Peter 2:7). This shows that you can be a believer and live in a compromised situation.

Abraham was walking with God, and the Lord wanted to spend time with him. But that wasn't the case with Lot. In fact, the visitors had to forcibly remove him from Sodom, like pulling a kid out of a toy store. He didn't want to leave, and his wife didn't want to go either. But one of the angels told him, "Flee for your lives! Don't look back, and don't stop anywhere in the plain! Flee to the mountains or you will be swept away!" (Genesis 19:17 NIV). Lot's wife did look back, and the Bible says she "became a pillar of salt" (verse 26 NIV). That is why Jesus warned, "Remember Lot's wife" (Luke 17:32).

WELCOME HOME, JESUS

Now we come to the question I raised earlier: Is Christ at home in your life? If He were to visit you today, would He be comfortable? Or, would He be ill at ease by the things you do and the decisions you make?

In his great little book called *My Heart—Christ's Home,* Robert Boyd Munger paints a picture of his heart being like a home where he invites Jesus to come and stay.

Think about that for a moment. What if there were suddenly a knock at your door tonight? You go to the door, and standing before you is Jesus Christ, the Son of God.

You invite Him in, and He begins walking through your house, looking around. He goes through your movie collection and checks out your DVDs. Then He goes over to your computer and takes a look at your browsing history. Next, He picks up your phone. He reads your e-mails and texts. You're feeling very uncomfortable at this point because there are some things you've been doing that you know you shouldn't be doing.

The truth is that Jesus actually does see all of those things. Are you doing something that would cause Him not to be at home in your heart? If so, you need to make a change. Maybe there are some skeletons in your closet that He needs to deal with. This is the time to surrender every corner of your life to Jesus Christ.

There is a show on television called *Restaurant: Impossible,* where the host, Robert Irvine, is contacted by people who own restaurants that are failing. They invite him to their restaurant, where he orders from their menu, looks at their facilities, and notes how the restaurant staff interacts. Then he will talk to each staff member and might even show them how to cook food properly. Then he has a team come in and refurbish the place. They tear everything apart, bring in new furniture and appliances, and completely transform the restaurant.

That is what Jesus wants to do in your heart.

He walks in and says, "Okay, we're going to make some changes here. This is coming out . . . that has to go. You need to change this area. . . ."

You're thinking, *This is not what I signed up for. I asked Christ to come into my life, and He is messing everything up. It's like a construction site!*

Just wait until He's done. Ultimately, you'll discover that whatever He removes from your life will be replaced by something far better.

Yes, there may be things that He wants to change. There may be relationships you're in right now that are dragging you down spiritually. Or even worse, you might be dragging someone else down spiritually.

There might be things you are looking at or listening to that are detrimental to your spiritual life. You are kind of like Lot, living in two worlds. You have too much of the world to be happy in the Lord, and too much of the Lord to be happy in the world. That is a foolish way to live your life.

Instead, your goal should be to be like Abraham, where the Lord is comfortable spending time, and lots of it, with you and likes being with you—and you like being with Him.

Is Christ at home in your heart? I'm not asking whether Christ *lives* in your heart. I'm asking whether He has settled down and is comfortable in your heart. Is He at home there?

That was Paul's prayer for the Ephesians. And that is my prayer for you too.

8

WALKING LESSONS

I, therefore, the prisoner of the Lord, beseech you to walk
worthy of the calling with which you were called.(Ephesians
4:1)

You probably don't remember taking your first steps as
a toddler. But if you're a parent, you almost certainly
remember when your children took their first steps. I remember
when my sons Christopher and Jonathan took theirs. It's a big
moment in the life of a parent when a child starts walking.

Part of the process of learning to walk is falling quite a few
times. Toddlers may grab a table or chair to pull themselves up,
and they bump their little heads. In fact, I remember Jonathan
bumping his head so many times in the same spot that it seemed
like he had a permanent bruise on his head when he was learning
to walk.

That is what happens in the Christian life as well. We fall
down a lot as we're learning to walk. But we should never give up.

Have you ever heard a toddler say, "Forget it! I'm not going
to try to walk anymore."

I haven't. But I have seen them get up and try again and
again. They always come back for more.

When we first come to Christ, those first few steps are hard. We may bump our heads here and there. We may even fall down a few times. But we need to get up and walk again.

At this point in the book of Ephesians, we have come to a new section. Ephesians could be divided into three sections: wealth, walk, and warfare, or live, love, and fight, as I like to call it. The first three chapters deal with our spiritual riches and wealth in Christ—all that God has given to us. And so far, we have learned about all the resources we have available for living this Christian life.

FROM PRACTICE TO PRINCIPLE

Now we are transitioning from positional to practical truth, from doctrine to duty, from creed to conduct, from exposition to exhortation, from practice to principle.

Right practice is always based on right principle.

Right living is based on right doctrine.

But some Christians don't like that word. They will say things like, *I'm not into doctrine; I just love the Lord!*

That's a sweet sentiment, but you need to be careful.

You just might end up loving the wrong lord.

Every Christian needs to love doctrine. Doctrine is just another word for teaching. As a believer, I need to know who God is. I need to know what God says so that I can worship Him intelligently as well as emotionally.

The Bible says, "God is Spirit, and those who worship Him must worship in spirit and truth" (John 4:24). Worship is not merely emotional; it's also intellectual. As I know more about God, I can worship Him more effectively.

Paul wrote to Timothy, "Watch your life and doctrine closely. Persevere in them, because if you do, you will save both yourself and your hearers" (1 Timothy 4:16 NIV). It's impossible to live the Christian life without knowing what God has given you. It's like trying to run your computer without power. Have you ever taken a trip but forgot to bring your power source? Forget about using your computer once the battery dies. Or, have you ever had your phone go dead when you were out somewhere and had no way of recharging it? It suddenly becomes a useless object that you're carrying around.

In the same way, we need to know what God's Word says. We need the right doctrine for right living.

Now we've arrived at the section where we will learn how to walk. Walking is a regular, consistent motion. It speaks of movement. It speaks of progress. And *walk* is an often-used term in the Bible to describe our lives in Christ:

> As you therefore have received Christ Jesus the Lord, so walk in Him. (Colossians 2:6)

> I say then: Walk in the Spirit, and you shall not fulfill the lust of the flesh. (Galatians 5:16)

> But if we walk in the light as He is in the light, we have fellowship with one another, and the blood of Jesus Christ His Son cleanses us from all sin. (1 John 1:7)

Here's what Paul says in Ephesians 4 about walking spiritually:

> I, therefore, the prisoner of the Lord, beseech you to walk worthy of the calling with which you were

called, with all lowliness and gentleness, with longsuffering, bearing with one another in love, endeavoring to keep the unity of the Spirit in the bond of peace. There is one body and one Spirit, just as you were called in one hope of your calling; one Lord, one faith, one baptism; one God and Father of all, who is above all, and through all, and in you all. (verses 1–6)

Again Paul begins by identifying himself as "the prisoner of the Lord." Of course, we know that Paul was in prison when he wrote this epistle, most likely in Rome. He wasn't writing these words from a nice beach in Greece, soaking up rays and sipping iced tea. Paul was in a place of discomfort, a place of hardship. Yet he still wrote words of great comfort and encouragement.

We need to understand that everything that happens in our lives is, as my friend Randy Alcorn says, "Father filtered." This means either God did it, or God allowed it. And many times we don't know why.

Paul owned the fact that he was in prison. He knew he was there because God allowed it.

Next, Paul gives a message that was burning on his heart: "I . . . beseech you to walk worthy of the calling with which you were called" (verse 1). The word *beseech* is a strong emotional term that means "to urge," "to plead," or even "to beg."

Paul was saying, "I am begging you to walk worthy of the calling with which you were called." That is the heart of a shepherd for his sheep.

We see this same heart when Paul referred to the believers in Galatia as "my little children, for whom I labor in birth again until Christ is formed in you" (Galatians 4:19). Paul was comparing himself to a woman giving birth, which is something we guys won't ever be able to completely wrap our minds around. But Paul was using it as an analogy, saying, in effect, "I don't want to see you come forward; I want to see you *go forward*. I don't want to see you just accept Christ; I want to see you grow in Christ, mature in Christ, develop your gifts from Christ, and then change the world for Christ."

Here in Ephesians 4, Paul was saying, "In light of what God has done for you, here's what should you be doing for Him."

PREPARATION FOR THE REAL WORLD

We want to bask in the glow of God's blessings, and that is a wonderful thing. But God blesses us so He can prepare us to face the real world. When we gather for worship, prayer, and Bible study, it's a time for us to be recharged, refreshed, and taught the Word of God. Something wonderful and supernatural happens when the church gathers together. The Bible promises that "where two or three are gathered together in My name, I am there in the midst of them" (Matthew 18:20).

While there is a place for listening to Bible teaching on the radio, downloading podcasts, or watching church services on television or the Internet, there is nothing quite like actually being in church and in fellowship with other Christians. Every believer needs to be actively involved in a local, Bible-teaching church.

When we come to worship, pray, and hear God's Word, it helps us see things differently. You can come into church with problems, and when you leave, your problems are effectively still with you. But worshiping and hearing the Word of God in church often will cause you to look at your problems differently. You may come with big problems and a small God. And you may leave with a big God and small problems. The problems are still the same, but you have a new way of looking at them.

We find an interesting passage in Psalm 73, where a man named Asaph was grappling with an age-old question: Why do the wicked prosper?

We could expand that by adding other questions such as these: Why do bad things happen? Why am I going through this hardship? Why am I suffering? Why did my loved one die? Our list of *why* questions goes on and on.

But then Asaph said, "When I tried to understand all this, it troubled me deeply *till I entered the sanctuary of God*; then I understood their final destiny" (verses 16–17 NIV, emphasis added).

You see, things changed for Asaph when he came to worship with God's people and heard God's Word. God gives us these blessings to help us live in the real world.

"WALK WORTHY"

Paul was saying, "You need to walk worthy." The word Paul used for *worthy* means "to balance the scales." But let's not misunderstand. God isn't saying we need to work really hard at being supergood Christians so we are worthy to approach Him. As I've already pointed out, we can approach God at any time because of the blood of Jesus Christ.

To "walk worthy" means something different altogether. To balance a scale, one side of the scale should be equal in weight to what is on the other side of the scale. That isn't to say we must do something equal to what God has done for us, because we never could.

But it is to say that we should give the proper response. God has done awesome, amazing things for us: choosing, loving, forgiving, adopting, sealing, and empowering us. Hence, there should be an equal response in which we do everything we can do in gratitude to Him. That is the idea Paul conveys here. He's saying there needs to be an appropriate response to what God has done for us.

So how do we walk worthy of the Lord?

As Much As Possible, Keep the Peace

Paul said, "Make every effort to keep yourselves united in the Spirit, binding yourselves together with peace" (Ephesians 4:3 NLT). Paul was not saying we need to create unity. Rather, we need to keep, or not break, the unity that's already there. When you become a Christian, you become a part of a family. You become a part of the church, the body of Christ. We are all in this together. Paul is saying, "Don't disrupt it. Don't cause division in it."

There are people who love to debate. They love to argue. They are always in a tiff about something. I don't have a problem having a doctrinal discussion with someone like this. At the same time, we are still supposed to love one another. It's possible to disagree agreeably.

God actually says one of the things He hates is "one who sows discord among brethren" (Proverbs 6:19). All that some people do is get into disputes with others. All they do is sow discord. Ironically, they think they're doing the work of God when, in fact, they aren't at all.

There is a place for theological distinctions. I have many close friendships with other pastors and leaders whom I don't agree with completely. You might be surprised to know how well we get along with each other, even though we have our disagreements. When we get together, we'll have a great time and realize that we never will resolve all those things. But we want to work together as the body of Christ.

Having said that, let me add this caveat. I cannot have unity with someone who does not believe that Jesus Christ is the only Son of God. I cannot have unity with someone who does not believe that Jesus Christ is the only way to God. I cannot have unity with someone who does not believe in the authority of the Scriptures. I believe that God's Word is inerrant; it is without error. I believe the Scriptures are breathed by God. As pastors and leaders, we might emphasize different things in our teaching, but we must hold these essential truths in common.

For example, there are different views on eschatology, the study of end-time events. I believe the Lord could come for believers at any time and that we'll be caught up in the Rapture before the tribulation period begins. There are some believers, however, who believe Christians will go through the tribulation period. I won't break fellowship with someone over that.

Then there are the differing views on baptism. Some Christians say you should be immersed when you're baptized. (I believe this because the word *baptize* means "immerse.") Others think sprinkling is sufficient for baptism. I would never break fellowship over that.

There are also different approaches to music. Some like hymns, and some like contemporary music. I would never break fellowship over something like that.

I love this often-quoted statement: "In essentials, unity; in nonessentials, liberty; in all things charity [love]."

In Romans 12, Paul wrote, "If it is possible, as much as depends on you, live peaceably with all men" (verse 18). I like this verse because Paul says, "If it is possible," which means it isn't always possible. There are some people you can't make peace with. If you've done everything you can to make peace with them and they still won't accept it, then move on. As much as it is possible, make peace with everyone.

And we need to maintain, as much as we can, unity with our fellow believers. How are we to keep this unity? Paul gives us the answer in the next verse: "Be completely humble and gentle; be patient, bearing with one another in love" (Ephesians 4:2 NIV).

Be Humble and Gentle

The New Living Translation puts it this way: "Always be humble and gentle. Be patient with each other, making allowance for each other's faults because of your love."

The Greeks influenced the Romans far more than the Romans influenced the Greeks. When the Romans conquered the Greeks, they essentially absorbed their culture. Thus, Greek philosophy permeated all of Rome.

The Greeks believed there was no place for humility. In fact, *humility* was a derogatory term. The Greek term for *humility* could be translated "low-mindedness" or "groveling servility." In other words, if you attempted to be a humble person, they would think of you as a little bit stupid and on the weak side. They didn't value humility; they valued strength, force, and conquering others.

So when the Scriptures talk about humility and meekness, many would dismiss this altogether. And many still do. Think about it: How many movies today celebrate forgiveness? Not many. How many movies celebrate vengeance and payback? A lot of them do.

For instance, there are the *Taken* movies starring Liam Neeson. In the first movie, Neeson's character, Bryan Mills, is on a cell phone with his daughter's kidnapper. Mills tells him, "If you are looking for ransom, I can tell you I don't have money. But what I do have are a very particular set of skills. Skills that I've acquired over a very long career. Skills that make me a nightmare for people like you."[1]

Yeah, the audience is thinking, *we want to see those skills!* That's what people like.

But then we have the Bible, which talks about humility, mercy, and forgiveness. And what I'm about to say might surprise you: It takes more strength to forgive than it does to take vengeance. In fact, it takes a great deal more strength.

The word used in the Bible for *meekness* would be best translated as "power under constraint." It was a word that typically referred to reigning in wild animals or a magnificent, powerful creature like a horse. With a bit and bridle, a horse will do what you want it to do. The idea is that of controlling something powerful—power under constraint. That is what meekness really means. Meekness is not weakness.

The strongest man who ever walked this earth was Jesus Christ. Pilate said of Jesus, "Behold the Man!" (John 19:5). Jesus was the man's man.

And who was the most humble man in history? Again, it's Jesus. He exercised meekness, power under constraint.

For example, when the soldiers came to arrest Him in the Garden of Gethsemane, Simon Peter pulled out his sword and started swinging away. But Jesus told him to put the sword away. Then He said, "Do you think that I cannot now pray to My Father, and He will provide Me with more than twelve legions of angels?" (Matthew 26:53).

In other words, "Peter, do you understand who I am? I could just say the word, and you would see a multitude of angels with swords drawn. But I have to go through this."

John's gospel includes this interesting detail about those who came to arrest Jesus:

> Jesus, knowing all that was going to happen to him, went out and asked them, "Who is it you want?"
>
> "Jesus of Nazareth," they replied.
>
> "I am he," Jesus said. (And Judas the traitor was standing there with them.)
>
> When Jesus said, "I am he," they drew back and fell to the ground. (John 18:4–6 NIV)

Just think of that—soldiers in armor, with swords and shields flashing, all falling on each other like a bunch of dominoes.

Jesus could have simply said, "I am . . . and you *were*. Bye."

But He was humble. He was meek. He exemplified power under constraint.

"That is fine," you may say. "That was Jesus."

Yes, it was Jesus. And guess what? The Bible says, "Let this mind be in you which was also in Christ Jesus" (Philippians 2:5). Or, as the New Living Translation puts it, "You must have the same attitude that Christ Jesus had."

In the same chapter, Paul defines what this looks like in real life:

> Then make me truly happy by agreeing wholeheartedly with each other, loving one another, and working together with one mind and purpose.

> Don't be selfish; don't try to impress others. Be
> humble, thinking of others as better than your-
> selves. Don't look out only for your own interests,
> but take an interest in others, too. (verses 2–4 NLT)

Imagine what would happen if we just applied those words
in our lives. Think how it would change your marriage. *Don't be
selfish. . . . Don't look out only for your own interests. . . .*

Think how it would change the way you work. *Don't be selfish; don't try to impress others. Be humble, thinking of others as
better than yourselves.* It would change everything.

Yes, we are to be meek. Having said that, I also want to point
out that we can be meek and strong at the same time. Moses was
described as the meekest man on the face of the earth; yet he fear-
lessly confronted Pharaoh in the name of the Lord. He also confronted the Israelites many times regarding their rebellion and sin.

The meek person is also capable of righteous anger and
action when needed, like when God's name is mocked or a
weaker person is being harmed.

Don't forget that Jesus, who submitted to the cross, also
drove the moneychangers out of the temple because they were
preying on the people instead of praying for the people. He used
a whip He had made himself. He overturned tables—and those
tables were heavy—to make His point.

Let's understand that meekness has strength as well.

Be Longsuffering

To walk worthy of our calling means that we also need to be
longsuffering. Coming back to verses 1 and 2 of Ephesians 4,
Paul wrote, "I . . . beseech you to walk worthy of the calling with

which you were called, with all lowliness and gentleness, with longsuffering."

To be longsuffering means to be "long tempered."

We need to be patient with God. He doesn't always move as quickly as we would like Him to.

Maybe you're single, and you're wondering, *When are you going to bring that person into my life?*

Maybe you want to serve the Lord in ministry, and you don't understand why He hasn't opened that door for you.

Know this: God has His plan, God has His way, and God has His timing. Sometimes you will be used by God, and sometimes the Lord will set you aside for a while because He needs to retool you a little, so to speak.

Take the story of Elijah, for example. He went into the court of Ahab, the king of Israel, and threw down the gauntlet: "As the Lord God of Israel lives, before whom I stand, there shall not be dew nor rain these years, except at my word" (1 Kings 17:1).

Then God told him to go to a brook called Cherith and just hang out there. That is where Elijah waited. He probably thought, *Why am I sitting by some dried-up stream in the middle of nowhere? I'm Elijah!* But God was getting him ready for the next step.

Moses had to be retrofitted, if you will, for the work that God would call him to do. He spent forty years in the desert, forty years in God's college getting his BD (backside of desert).

Saul of Tarsus was a brilliant man, schooled under Gamaliel. He was a great orator and one of the greatest teachers of all time. But after Saul was converted, the Lord had to get him ready for his new work that would go along with his new name: the apostle Paul.

Be patient with God.

And be patient with people too. This is difficult, because people can try our patience, can't they? That is because we are very self-centered, generally. Sin always puts us at the center of everything. We wonder, *How will this will affect me? What's in it for me? What can you do for me? What about my needs?* The problem is that we don't think of others and the effect on others.

People want to selfishly do their own thing. If the marriage isn't working, they just dissolve it. Never mind what the Bible says. Never mind the children.

If they want to be unfaithful to their spouse, they go for it. If they want to have sex before marriage, they do that too. They think, *What does it matter what the Bible says?*

The apostle Paul confronted a problem like that in the Corinthian church. Corinth was a very wicked area that was known for sexual perversion. Incredibly, the believers in Corinth actually were boasting about how they let an immoral man stay in their church. He was sleeping with his father's wife (not his mother, but his father's wife).

Paul told them, "Your boasting about this is terrible. Don't you realize that this sin is like a little yeast that spreads through the whole batch of dough? Get rid of the old 'yeast' by removing this wicked person from among you" (1 Corinthians 5:6–7 nlt). One person affects another person. We need to think of others.

WHAT SETS CHRISTIANITY APART

We also need to think of the church as a whole. In Ephesians 4, Paul continues,

There is one body and one Spirit, just as you were
called in one hope of your calling; one Lord, one
faith, one baptism; one God and Father of all,
who is above all, and through all, and in you all.
(verses 4–6)

There is one body of believers, the church. It's comprised of
different nations, cultures, races, and theological distinctions.
But we know the church is universal because one day in Heaven,
people that are worshiping God will have come from all around
the world.

Revelation 7:9 says, "After this I saw a vast crowd, too great
to count, from every nation and tribe and people and language,
standing in front of the throne and before the Lamb. They were
clothed in white robes and held palm branches in their hands"
(NLT). In Heaven, people from everywhere will be worshiping
God. Everyone will be reached, including the so-called unreach-
able nations. God will reach them. There is one church.

There is one Spirit, and He is the Holy Spirit who convicts us
initially. He convinces us of our need for Jesus, He seals us when
we believe, and then He empowers us for service.

There is one Lord, and that one Lord is Jesus Christ. Acts 4:12
says, "Salvation is found in no one else, for there is no other name
under heaven given to mankind by which we must be saved"
(NIV). There is one faith, and that is the Christian faith that is based
on the life, death, and resurrection of Jesus Christ. Jude 3 speaks
of "the faith which was once for all delivered to the saints."

By the way, in the same verse, Jude tells us to "contend
earnestly for the faith." We should be able to defend our faith.
The Bible says we should "always be ready to give a defense to
everyone who asks you a reason for the hope that is in you, with
meekness and fear" (1 Peter 3:15).

Right after I became a Christian, I was growing dramatically in my faith. I made a complete break with all of my buddies who did drugs, and I started going to church and reading the Bible. I was like a sponge, soaking up everything.

I had a buddy, also named Gregg, whom I had known since elementary school. We were best friends, and when I became I Christian, I assured Gregg that I wouldn't become one of those fanatical Christians. I would still be his same old buddy Greg. I said, "You will never see Greg Laurie walking around, carrying a Bible, and saying, 'Praise the Lord!' It won't happen."

Two weeks later, I was in Newport Beach talking to people on the street about what it was to know Christ. As I was walking down the street, carrying my Bible, I saw Gregg walking toward me. Before I could catch myself, I looked at him and said, "Praise the Lord!"

We both laughed because it was so ironic.

"Gregg," I told him, "what can I say? I know I told you I would not walk around with a Bible saying, 'Praise the Lord!' But Gregg, Jesus is real and He has changed me. Let me tell you what He has done for me."

As Gregg listened, there was a guy standing nearby who was eavesdropping on our conversation. He walked over and said, "I have a few questions for you, Christian."

I thought, *Okay, I'm ready for anything. I've been a Christian for two whole weeks.*

He fired off about five tough questions, and my mind went blank. I didn't know the answer.

Gregg looked at me and said, "Yeah, Laurie, what about that?"

I was humiliated. But I thought, *Next time, I'm going to be ready*. And then I started studying like crazy.

We should be able to defend our faith.

In contrast to many other faiths, we believe in one God. *There is one body and one Spirit . . . one Lord, one faith, one baptism; one God and Father of all.* Christianity is monotheistic: we believe in one God (see Deuteronomy 6:4). At the same time, this one God reveals himself in three persons: Father, Son, and Holy Spirit.

On the other hand, Hinduism is polytheistic. Hindus believe in many gods. In fact, they believe in gods and goddesses. The same is true of those in the Hare Krishna movement. Buddhists, however, do not worship any god or gods. Buddhists believe that a person has countless rebirths, which inevitably includes suffering. They seek to end these rebirths.

Muslims also believe in one god, but it is not the same God whom Christians believe in. They believe in Allah, while Christians believe in the Lord God—*Yahweh*, Jehovah. It is wrong to say that Muslims and Christians worship the same god. We don't.

There are distinctions in the various religions. So when someone says, "All religions teach the same thing," he or she is actually saying, "I don't know what I'm talking about."

All religions don't teach the same thing. Hindus acknowledge multitudes of gods and goddesses. Buddhists say there is no deity. Muslims believe in a powerful but unknowable god. But Christians believe in one God and one Father who is both knowable and approachable. There is "one Lord, one faith, one baptism; one God and Father of all."

LONG OBEDIENCE IN THE SAME DIRECTION

We need to spend our time getting to know God and walking with Him. And walking implies effort and having direction with a destination in mind. We should want to make progress.

Following Jesus is, as one person said, "long obedience in the same direction."[2]

Some people think they need to be born again and again and again. They come to church waiting for that big breakthrough moment. But they had that breakthrough moment at the time of their conversion. Now they need long obedience in the same direction.

Yes, God will fill you with His Spirit. Yes, God will cause your faith to grow. But stop looking for that emotional experience and just walk with God.

The Bible says, "The just shall live by faith" (Romans 1:17). It doesn't say the just will live by feelings or emotional experiences. Those come and go. Walking with God, however, involves faith, trust, and growing in your relationship with Him.

Maybe in your spiritual walk you've fallen so many times that you have a permanent bruise like my son Jonathan had as a toddler. Keep trying. Don't give up. And when you fall, realize that you can't get up on your own. You need the Lord to pull you up.

Remember the story of Simon Peter when he got out of the boat and walked on water? When he started to sink, he cried out to Jesus, who immediately reached down and pulled him up.

Jesus will do the same for you. You just need to call out to Him.

9

YOUR PLACE IN THE CHURCH

However, he has given each one of us a special gift through the generosity of Christ.(Ephesians 4:7)

Have you ever received a gift you didn't like? Maybe you opened it and tried to look happy. But in reality, you weren't happy at all.

Sometimes people give us things we don't really want, like fruitcakes. I have a theory that only one fruitcake exists on Earth, and we have been redistributing it for hundreds of years. Think about it: Have you ever seen two fruitcakes side by side? That's because there actually is only one. We just keep regifting it.

I always include gift receipts with the gifts I give. I'll tell the recipient, "Here's where I bought it. I don't know whether I chose the right thing, so I'd love it if you would take it back and get whatever you want, because I want you to be happy."

Sometimes someone will come back and say, "How do you like my shoes?"

"They're nice. Why do you ask?"

"Well, you bought them for me."

"Great! Happy birthday!"

The gift that God gives always will be the right one. You won't want to return it. It's a gift suited for you, and it's always appropriate. God personally chooses the gifts that He gives us.

Sometimes it may not make sense as to why He chooses certain gifts for certain people. The thought of my being a teacher of any kind would have been a laugh-out-loud joke to everyone who taught me throughout my school years. I was the worst student ever. To think that God called me to be a teacher and preacher seems almost crazy. That's why He gets the glory.

Whether the gift makes sense to us or not, God expects us to use it. And in Ephesians 4, Paul tells us a little about the gifts of the Spirit and why the Lord gave them to us.

THE IMPORTANCE OF THE CHURCH

Let me just say that I thank God for the church. People are quick to criticize the church, put down the church, and complain about the church. But there is nothing this world or culture offers that even comes close to who we are as followers of Jesus, and what we can have together.

The problem is that sometimes we don't really understand the role of the church or our place in it. And some people almost treat church like going to a movie.

"What time does the movie start?"

"It starts at 7:00."

"Let's get there late, because they are just going to roll a bunch of trailers first."

They come in late, watch the feature presentation, and leave as soon as it's over, before the credits roll.

Then they'll bring the same cavalier attitude when they come to church. They think of worship like the movie trailers. But worship isn't a warm-up act; it's an essential part. Worship is prayer set to song. We need to think about church in a different way. It isn't a place to simply hear a message, sing a few songs, say hello to good friends, and then go home (though it includes these things). It's a family gathering.

Every believer needs to be a part of the church for a number of reasons. Every believer needs a pastor, someone who is a spiritual leader in his or her life. Every believer needs a place to be spiritually fed. And every believer needs a place to be accountable.

That is the problem with church hopping. Someone goes Sunday mornings to one church and Sunday nights to another church. Then he or she goes to four more churches. That isn't a good idea.

If someone is visiting our church, I don't want to bring them into our congregation if they are part of another body of believers. What I want to see them do is to get involved in their own church and engage. When they don't do that, they miss out on all the church can be.

Understand, it is not all about you. Church is not there only to serve you. As you mature and grow, you should start serving others. That is part of God's objective, which we'll see in the verses we're about to study.

Already in this epistle, Paul has gone into great depth to tell us what God has done for us. Now he effectively tells us what we should do in response to that. That is why Ephesians 4 begins, "Therefore I, a prisoner for serving the Lord, beg you to lead a life worthy of your calling, for you have been called by God" (verse 1 NLT). Whenever you see the word *therefore*, always find out what it is there for. It is always drawing from what has been previously said. Paul already has told us about the riches we have in Christ. Now, here's how it plays out in our day-to-day living.

Before we look at some gifts of the Spirit, I want to contrast them with what we would call talents. Different people are born with different talents. Some are artistic. Some are musical. Some have more of a mechanical mind. Some are great at crunching numbers. But every person has been born with certain abilities and talents.

When we talk about the gifts of the Spirit, however, we are talking about something different altogether. This is a gift from Heaven that God supernaturally instills in our lives that may not even be related to a natural talent we already have. This is different from a talent (which you also want to use for the glory of God).

Verse 7 says that "he has given each one of us a special gift through the generosity of Christ" (NLT). This is reinforced by what Paul wrote in Romans: "We, being many, are one body in Christ, and individually members of one another. Having then gifts differing according to the grace that is given to us, let us use them" (12:5–6).

God has given us these gifts, and we are to use them.

What we want to avoid is envying someone else's spiritual gifts. There are pastors who wish they were rock stars, worship leaders who wish they were pastors, evangelists who wish they were pastors, and pastors who wish they were evangelists. How about just being thankful for whatever gifts God has given us and developing and using them for His glory?

I remember one Christmas as a kid when I was very happy with what I had received—that is, until my friend got something that I really wanted: a plastic skin diver toy. The little battery-operated diver sank to the bottom of the pool and had bubbles that poured out of him. (Understand, this was 1960s technology.) I thought it was the coolest thing I'd ever seen. And suddenly I was no longer happy with any of the gifts I had received.

We can do the same thing as Christians. We see someone with a certain spiritual gift, and we think, *I want their gift. I wish I was called to do what they are called to do.* No, each of us is supposed to do what God has called us to. As Paul pointed out in 1 Corinthians, "It is the one and only Spirit who distributes all these gifts. He alone decides which gift each person should have" (12:11 NLT). In the same chapter, Paul also wrote, "Now concerning spiritual gifts, brethren, I do not want you to be ignorant" (verse 1). Yet I think there is more ignorance on this topic than any other when it comes to living the Christian life. We just don't seem to understand how these gifts work.

I believe that one reason we are resistant to the idea of gifts of the Spirit is because we've seen such crazy abuse of them. It seems like whenever we see someone weird (and they always seem to be on television) who claims that the Holy Spirit is really at work, people are doing things like rolling around on the ground, barking like dogs, or engaging in so-called holy laughter.

Meanwhile, nonbelievers are saying, "I don't want to be a Christian if that is what I'm supposed to do."

Or, more to the point, "I don't want that if that is what the work of the Holy Spirit is."

No, that is not the Holy Spirit. That is just a bunch of weird people doing weird things, and it has nothing to do with the Holy Spirit of God.

When we recoil from this, we're throwing out the good with the bad. I believe there are gifts of the Spirit. And I believe they're available for believers today. In fact, the Bible says, "Christ was confirmed in you, so that you come short in no gift, eagerly waiting for the revelation of our Lord Jesus Christ" (1 Corinthians 1:7).

One position on spiritual gifts is held by cessationists, who don't believe the gifts of the Spirit are for today. Or, they might believe that certain gifts are for today, such as teaching and evangelism, while others like "sign" gifts or miracles are not, because now we have the Bible.

I am all for the Bible, obviously. But one of the signs of the last days is there will be satanically energized times. Don't you think we need all of the power we can get to live for Christ? I think so.

Paul said in 1 Corinthians 14:1 that we should "desire spiritual gifts." That word *desire* could be translated "earnestly want and cultivate." It's vital that we desire these gifts, discover what they are, and if we have them, to not let them lie dormant. Otherwise, we might find ourselves quenching the Holy Spirit.

The Bible tells us, "Do not quench the Spirit" (1 Thessalonians 5:19). *Quench* means "to extinguish." If you're camping or at the beach and have a fire going for the night, when it's time to leave, you pour water on it. Some put sand or dirt on it. You're extinguishing, or quenching, that fire.

When God gives you a spiritual gift and you say, "No, I don't want that gift. I don't want to do that thing for God," that is quenching the Holy Spirit.

God wants this power for us in our Christian lives, and we should want it too.

GIFTS CHRIST GAVE TO THE CHURCH

In verse 11 of Ephesians 4, Paul identifies four groups of people as "gifts Christ gave to the church": 1) apostles, 2) prophets, 3) evangelists, and 4) pastors and teachers.

Apostles

Let's start with apostles. The word *apostle* means "a sent one," or literally, one who is sent on a mission. In its primary and most technical sense, *apostle* is used in the New Testament only regarding the Twelve who were called by Jesus. Judas Iscariot, who disqualified himself for obvious reasons, was replaced by Matthias (see Acts 1:15–26).

But then along comes the apostle Paul. Though he wasn't one of the original Twelve who walked with Christ, he described himself as "an apostle of Jesus Christ, by the commandment of God our Savior and the Lord Jesus Christ" (1 Timothy 1:1). He met the requirements of apostleship in that he saw the risen Lord and was chosen by Jesus (see Acts 9:1–19; 1 Corinthians 9:1).

These apostles, these men of God whom we read about in the New Testament, spoke the words given to them by God. When Peter spoke and wrote, that was Scripture. When Paul spoke and wrote, that was the Word of God. They weren't perfect men. But they were men whom God called and moved through in a unique way. He breathed His Word into them and through them (see 2 Peter 1:20–21), and that is what we regard as the Scriptures today.

What about modern-day apostles, however? There are some people who claim to be apostles or even introduce themselves as an apostle. I'm a little nervous about that because it's almost as though they are saying, "I am an apostle, and you cannot question my word."

There is no preacher whom you should not question, including me. Any preacher can misrepresent God. Any preacher can be in error theologically. Don't believe something because I have said it or another preacher has said it. Follow the example of the Bereans. They actually checked up on Paul's teaching. In Acts 17:11 we read, "Now the Berean Jews were of more noble character than those in Thessalonica, for they received the message with great eagerness and examined the Scriptures every day to see if what Paul said was true" (NIV). If they were checking out Paul, then shouldn't we be checking out so-called modern-day apostles?

The Bible warns there will be false apostles in the end times. Paul wrote to the Corinthian believers about such imposters, saying,

> These people are false apostles. They are deceitful workers who disguise themselves as apostles of Christ. But I am not surprised! Even Satan disguises himself as an angel of light. So it is no wonder that his servants also disguise themselves as servants of righteousness. In the end they will get the punishment their wicked deeds deserve. (2 Corinthians 11:12–15 NLT)

That is the negative; now let's come back to the positive. I don't believe there are apostles today on the level of the original Twelve. No one will speak authoritatively to the extent their words will become Scripture and new sections will be added to our Bible. That is finished. That is complete.

But someone could have an apostle-like ministry. They may be gifted and called by God to plant churches. They may be missionaries who go to a certain place and do a work, and then they move on and do another work. That is apostolic in a broad sense.

Now let's move on to our next group: prophets.

Prophets

Apostles and prophets are different. A prophet is not sent on a mission per se. In general, a prophet has a message. Isaiah, Daniel, and Ezekiel all were prophets. In many cases, they predicted the future.

When someone who claims to be a prophet says they're speaking for the Lord, here's how to tell whether that person is indeed a prophet. If what that person says actually happens, then maybe he or she is a prophet. But if what that person says doesn't happen, then he or she is a false prophet.

Deuteronomy 18:21–22 says, "You may say to yourselves, 'How can we know when a message has not been spoken by the Lord?' If what a prophet proclaims in the name of the Lord does not take place or come true, that is a message the Lord has not spoken. That prophet has spoken presumptuously, so do not be alarmed" (NIV). Again, just as there will be false apostles in the end times, the Bible warns there will be false prophets as well (see Matthew 24:11, 24; Mark 13:22; 1 John 4:1).

Yet there is a place where God can speak through you. Another translation of *prophesy* means "to bubble forth." There have been times when the Lord will give me some words that I never had considered personally. I hadn't prepared those remarks. They just seem to come from Heaven, not from me.

Have you ever had someone say, "I'm struggling with this," and all of a sudden you begin sharing things with them? It's so exciting that you want to take notes on yourself!

You think, *This is amazing! I didn't come up with this.*

While I don't think we have prophets in the sense of an Old Testament prophet who predicts the future, I believe there can be a ministry today where the Lord can speak through you, giving you those words that seem to "bubble forth."

Now let's look at evangelists.

Evangelists

A literal definition of *evangelist* would be "bearers of good news." Historically, God has raised up many great evangelists. We can go back, of course, to the apostles. Certainly, Peter was a gifted evangelist. Paul was a great evangelist. Philip is uniquely identified in the New Testament as an evangelist.

In American history, we have George Whitfield, who preached to thousands of people without a microphone. It was said that people in crowds as large as thirty thousand could hear him. Amazing.

Next there were people like Billy Sunday and of course, D. L. Moody.

Today, when we hear the word *evangelist*, the one we all think of immediately is Billy Graham, who has been so gifted by God.

Here's something you may not know about evangelists. You don't have to be a preacher to be an evangelist. Some of the most effective evangelists I have heard don't have pulpits. They don't hold crusades. They don't do special meetings. They simply have been gifted by God to articulate the gospel.

An evangelist is a man or a woman who has been given a special gift by God to articulate their faith. I don't know why some people seem to have that ability more than others. I just recognize it as a gift.

I will watch them and think, *That is the gift of evangelism. They have that gift.*

When they speak, somehow people get it. They understand it. This is a very important gift. I've also found that those who are called as evangelists often have a gift of encouraging the church, exhorting the church.

This brings us to the final group: pastor-teachers.

Pastor-Teachers

In the original language, the words *pastors* and *teachers* in verse 11 would be one category. If you are called to be a pastor, then you need to be a teacher. What is the objective of a pastor? It is to feed the flock of God, the Bible says, and to declare the whole counsel of God.

Sometimes I'm asked what I think the greatest need is in the church is today. As I travel and speak in different churches, I would say the greatest need in the church today is for clear, biblical exposition. I believe this is sorely lacking. I think we have probably the most biblically illiterate generation of all time right now. Even people who attend church don't have, in many cases, even a basic working knowledge of the Scriptures and of the Word of God. That is why it's so important for a pastor-teacher to teach the Word of God, chapter by chapter, verse by verse. This is what we are commanded by God to do.

Paul wrote to Timothy, "Preach the word; be prepared in season and out of season; correct, rebuke and encourage—with great patience and careful instruction" (2 Timothy 4:2 NLT). Then Paul went on to explain why we should do this: "For the time will come when people will not put up with sound doctrine. Instead, to suit their own desires, they will gather around them a great number of teachers to say what their itching ears want to hear. They will turn their ears away from the truth and turn aside to myths" (verse 3 NLT). As a pastor-teacher, I'm not here to entertain; I'm here to simply teach God's Word to you, to make it as understandable as I can, and to proclaim the gospel.

I think when people go to church, they want the preacher to preach. They don't want a stand-up comedian. They don't want a psychologist. They don't want a social activist. I've heard some preachers refer to themselves as a "Life Coach".

I am happy to be called to be a preacher and I make no apology for it. A preacher should be a preacher and thank God for that calling. A preacher should open the Bible and tell people what it says. That is what I think we need in churches today.

At Harvest Christian Fellowship where I pastor, we offer theology without apology. And at our services, you can expect us to open the Bible and have a Bible study. People will develop an appetite for what you feed them.

Paul explains in Ephesians 4 that "Christ himself gave the apostles, the prophets, the evangelists, the pastors and teachers, *to equip his people for works of service*, so that the body of Christ may be built up" (verses 11–12 NIV, emphasis added).

The role of a pastor-teacher is not just to teach people; it is to train and equip them. As of this writing, we have about fifteen hundred people at Harvest Christian Fellowship in Riverside actively involved in serving the Lord as volunteers. They might go on a short-term mission trip, serve at the Fred Jordan Mission on Skid Row in Los Angeles, work as an usher at one of our services, or serve as a counselor. The list goes on. But I'll tell you this much: these are blessed people. A big church becomes a small church when you get involved.

This is why it's so important to find out what your gifts are and start using them. And sometimes figuring out what they are is as simple as the process of elimination. When I was a brand-new Christian, I volunteered to do everything. I found out very quickly what I wasn't so great at. But sometimes, it's a matter of discovering what we aren't called to do that will help us discover what we are called to do. So just volunteer.

The Greek word for *equip* in verse 12 refers to something being restored to its original condition. If you've ever seen a classic car that has been restored to perfection cruising down the road, you have to admit it's a thing of beauty.

That is what *equip* means here. It is getting something back to its original condition so it will do what it was meant to do originally. By the way, the word is also a medical term used in regard to the setting of bones. The idea is to find out what God has gifted you to do and then start serving in that capacity.

THE GIFTS GOD GIVES TO HIS CHILDREN

In Romans 12, we find a list of the gifts God gives:

> In his grace, God has given us different gifts for
> doing certain things well. So if God has given you
> the ability to prophesy, speak out with as much
> faith as God has given you. If your gift is serv-
> ing others, serve them well. If you are a teacher,
> teach well. If your gift is to encourage others,
> be encouraging. If it is giving, give generously.
> If God has given you leadership ability, take the
> responsibility seriously. And if you have a gift for

showing kindness to others, do it gladly. (verses 6–8 NLT)

Certain phrases seem to rise to the surface: *serve them well, teach well, give generously, take this responsibility seriously, do it gladly.*

Let's consider a few of these gifts.

Exhortation

The gift of exhortation is an interesting gift. To *exhort* means "to motivate, stimulate, and excite." It also implies correction. Where a teacher will tell you how to do something, someone with a gift of exhortation will make you want to do it well. That is an important gift.

I don't want to say that exhorting someone is like being a spiritual cheerleader, because that trivializes it. A person with the gift of exhortation might tell you, "I see this ability in you, and I think you can do this thing. You have to go out there right now, just take a step of faith, and see what will happen."

Somehow, after their little pep talk, you actually want to go out and give it a go. That is the gift of exhortation. It is motivating. It is stimulating. It is encouraging. And sometimes exhorting is also correcting.

Sometimes we are exhorted in church. Hebrews 10:24–25 says, "And let us consider one another in order to stir up love and good works, not forsaking the assembling of ourselves together, as *is* the manner of some, but exhorting one another, and so much the more as you see the Day approaching."

When Paul and Barnabas visited the churches in Lystra, Iconium, and Antioch, "they encouraged them to continue in the faith, reminding them that we must suffer many hardships to enter the Kingdom of God" (Acts 14:22 NLT). When circumstances are bad, when we're having family problems or health problems or financial problems, we can come to church and hear teaching where we receive encouragement to press on, encouragement that God is faithful. We need that. We need people in the church with the gift of exhortation.

Giving

Then we have the gift of giving. Romans 12:8 says that if this is your spiritual gift, "give generously" (NLT).

Someone may say, "Well, I don't have that gift. I'm not rich enough."

You don't have to be rich to have the gift of giving.

By the way, whether or not this is your spiritual gift, every believer should give regularly and faithfully of their finances to the Lord. Many believers haven't learned this discipline in their lives. God doesn't ask for your money because He needs your money. God asks you to give in this area because He knows that often it's a real indication of the level of your commitment.

Jesus said, "For where your treasure is, there your heart will be also" (Matthew 6:21).

He also said, "It is more blessed to give than to receive" (Acts 20:35). Kids tend to think it is more blessed to receive than give. But as we get a little older and a little more mature, we start discovering the joy of giving.

Every believer should give. In fact, there is an interesting passage in Malachi 3 where God says Israel had robbed Him. We wouldn't think of taking money out of the offering and putting it in our pocket. Yet God said the people had robbed Him in their tithes and offerings. Then He challenges them to put Him to the test: "'Bring the whole tithe into the storehouse, that there may be food in my house. Test me in this,' says the Lord Almighty, 'and see if I will not throw open the floodgates of heaven and pour out so much blessing that there will not be room enough to store it'" (verse 10 NIV). Many have never put God to the test in this sense. They've never given to the Lord. And they're missing out. We're told in 1 Corinthians that when we come together to worship the Lord, we should always bring our offering: "On the first day of each week, you should each put aside a portion of the money you have earned" (16:2 NLT). The offering should not come as a surprise to us. Having said that, there is a specific spiritual gift of giving. I've met people who have very little, yet they are so generous that it's mind-blowing. (I've also met people who are very well off financially, yet they are so stingy, it's unbelievable.) I've seen people who will give out of what God has given them—and how the Lord blesses them. That is the gift of giving.

Then there is the gift of showing mercy and kindness.

Mercy and Kindness

Coming back to Romans 12, we read, "And if you have a gift for showing kindness to others, do it gladly" (verse 8 NLT). Some people have an extraordinary, supernatural ability from God to show mercy, compassion, and kindness to those in need. I have seen them. I have seen them in hospitals. I have seen them in convalescent homes. I have seen them on the streets. And I have seen them do amazing things. I think that is a gift from God. There is just something about them that brings comfort and help to people who are in need.

If you're in the hospital, I don't think you necessarily need a pastor-teacher. That would be okay. But someone with a gift of mercy probably would do a lot of good for you, someone to hold your hand and say, "I'm really sorry you're going through this. Let's pray. Is there anything I can do for you?" There is something about them that draws you out. That is a gift from God.

WHY SPIRITUAL GIFTS?

Each of the spiritual gifts God gives is different, but one isn't more important than another.

What are your gifts? Have you discovered them yet? If you have discovered them, are you using them? We all have a part to play. Each gift matters.

Coming back to Ephesians 4, we see the reason God has given the gifts of the Spirit:

> Then we will no longer be infants, tossed back and forth by the waves, and blown here and there by every wind of teaching and by the cunning and craftiness of people in their deceitful scheming. Instead, speaking the truth in love, we will grow to become in every respect the mature body of him who is the head, that is, Christ. (verses 14–15 NIV)

God gives the gifts of the Spirit so we will grow up. When we start out as Christians, we're like babies. In fact, in his first epistle, John addresses little children, young men, and fathers. That is the progression when you come to Christ. You start out as a little child, then you become a young man (or woman) in the faith, and then you become a father (or mother) in the faith who passes it on to the next generation.

Just as little children are fickle and can go from laughing to crying in a millisecond, young believers have high highs and low lows as well. They can change their opinions very quickly. They're influenced by the last preacher they heard or the last book they read. They don't have a consistent theology yet.

That is why we need to be in church hearing the Word of God, developing our gifts, and developing a consistent theology. That way, we no longer will be like children.

Another trait of young children is they love exciting new things. Christians can be that way too sometimes. They want novelty. They want gimmicks. They tire of the Word of God. We want to grow past that.

It is one thing if you have been a Christian for six months or a year. But when you have known the Lord for five or ten years and are still acting like a baby, I have two words for you: *grow up!*

It is time to start digging into the Scriptures for yourself. God has given you spiritual gifts He has chosen them specifically for you. It is time to find out what they are, develop them, and start using them.

That is what Hebrews 5:12 is saying: "You have been believers so long now that you ought to be teaching others. Instead, you need someone to teach you again the basic things about God's word. You are like babies who need milk and cannot eat solid food" (NLT). If you haven't been a Christian for very long, there is nothing wrong with that. You need to continue to grow. You need to be around mature Christians who will help you grow spiritually. Kids realize they're kids. So if you're a young Christian, recognize that about yourself and spend time with people who are more mature in the faith than you are.

Younger Christians are vulnerable. That is why Christians who are more mature should be seeking out Christians who are newer in the faith and start spending time with them, praying for them, having Bible studies with them, and going to church with them. Seek to integrate new Christians into the church as quickly as possible so they don't fall through the cracks. They are vulnerable, as Paul pointed out: "Then [they] will no longer be infants, tossed back and forth by the waves, and blown here and there by every wind of teaching and by the cunning and craftiness of people in their deceitful scheming" (Ephesians 4:14 NIV).

LOOK OUT FOR EACH OTHER

There is a devil, and he "walks about like a roaring lion, seeking whom he may devour" (1 Peter 5:8).

How do we protect ourselves? We find the answer in verse 15 of Ephesians 4: "Instead, we will speak the truth in love, growing in every way more and more like Christ, who is the head of his body, the church" (NLT). The word for *speak* here means "profess." Perhaps the best translation would be, "Have or hold the truth in love."

Sometimes when people tell the truth they don't do it in love. They feel they should just blurt out whatever comes into their mind. For example, they might walk up to someone and say, "You are really fat."

That may be true. But is that the right thing to say to a person?

Just because something is true doesn't mean we need to say it. We should speak the truth in love.

Sometimes you may point out something that is wrong in another person's life, but you didn't do it lovingly. Technically, what you were saying was true, but you didn't use tact. Because of that, he or she was resistant to what you said, and it was completely ineffective.

On the other hand, we can be loving and not speak the truth. If I know someone is destroying their life and I don't tell them the truth, that also is a deficiency.

To speak the truth in love does not mean that we smile on all other views and never disagree, criticize, or reject another viewpoint. If I say that a certain group of people is a cult, I am doing so because I want to warn Christians.

Some might say, "Well, that is not very loving of you to say that certain groups like Mormons are cults."

When I use the word *cult*, I don't mean it in a mean way, necessarily. I mean it to say that Mormonism, for example, is not orthodox Christianity. They believe that one day they can become gods. They believe that Adam was a god. They believe that one day they will rule their own planets. That is not orthodox Christianity. They have another book they hold equal to the Scriptures, *The Book of Mormon*.

When you are an orthodox, committed Christian, the only authority is Scripture and Scripture alone.

So when people think it isn't very loving to identify certain groups as cults, I think the very opposite is true. I think it is loving.

Let's say, for instance, that some young kids set up a lemonade stand, got confused, and instead of selling lemonade, they were selling strychnine. People were drinking it and dying.

You became aware of it and say, "Shut down this lemonade stand. Don't anybody else drink it."

"Well, that is not very loving," someone says. "These kids will get their feelings hurt."

No, they are selling poison. You are going to warn people because you don't want them to die.

In the same way, I have a responsibility as a pastor to tell the truth. We have responsibilities as Christians to tell the truth. The streams of love and grace must always flow within the banks of truth.

Sometimes we will turn a blind eye to sin in a fellow Christian's life. We think, *I don't want to be judgmental. I just want to be loving.*

We need to be loving by speaking the truth in love and trying to help them get on the right track where they need to be.

"Well, I just want to err on the side of love and grace," someone might say.

How about if we don't err at all? How about if we show love and grace and speak the truth?

Again, love flows within the banks of truth.

And when it comes to brand-new believers, we must be especially careful to do everything we can to protect them.

EVERYONE MATTERS

Having said that, if you have known the Lord for a while, it is time to grow up. That is what Paul tells us in verse 16 of Ephesians 4: "Under his direction, the whole body is fitted together perfectly, and each part in its own special way helps the other parts, so that the whole body is healthy and growing and full of love" (tlb). We all have a part to play in the church. Everyone matters. The younger believer is there to motivate and encourage the older believer. The older believer is there to help stabilize the younger believer.

Some believers have public roles. Take Saul of Tarsus, for example. One of the most notorious people around at the time of the early church, he hunted down and killed Christians. But he was converted by Jesus Himself on the Damascus Road and transformed into the apostle Paul. We thank God for the Pauls of the world, those whom God raises up in a public way.

Some believers have roles behind the scenes. Shortly after Saul's conversion, the Lord directed a man named Ananias to go and pray for him. Later, the Lord directed a man named Barnabas to take Paul under his wing and vouch for him within the church, because many didn't believe he was actually a Christian. They thought it was some kind of a ruse.

We can't all be apostle Pauls. Sometimes we need to be an Ananias. Sometimes we need to be a Barnabas. You may not be the next Billy Graham, but you may be the best person to help nurture the next Billy Graham. We all have a role to play. Let's find that role.

Finding your place in the church will change your entire worship experience. Stop coming as a spectator. Start coming as a participant. Become a part of the family of God.

Do it.

You'll be glad you did.

10

WHAT MAKES GOD SAD

Do not grieve the Holy Spirit of God, by whom you were sealed for the day of redemption.(Ephesians 4:30)

I have discovered that women have a secret weapon guys are helpless against. Kids sometimes have it too—especially little girls. And what is that secret weapon?

Crying.

As a guy, when you see the tears well up in her eyes, the party is over. Even if you're having an argument and know without a doubt that you're right and she's dead wrong, you start apologizing. The same goes with kids, especially little girls. (I have firsthand knowledge of this because I have four granddaughters.) Whatever they want, you will do it, as long as they stop crying. I am fully convinced it's their secret weapon.

But there is something worse than seeing that special woman or girl in your life cry, as difficult as that might be to imagine. What's even worse is bringing sorrow to the Holy Spirit.

"But Greg," someone might say, "I thought the Holy Spirit was like some kind of force. How do you make a force sad?"

No, the Holy Spirit is not a force. The Holy Spirit is a part of the Trinity. God is a triune being: Father, Son, and Holy Spirit. The work of the Holy Spirit, according to Jesus, is to convict and convince us of our sin (see John 16:8–11).

What's more, the Holy Spirit can be specifically sinned against. In Ephesians 4, we are told, "Do not grieve the Holy Spirit of God, by whom you were sealed for the day of redemption" (verse 30). It's worth noting that *grieve* means "to make sad or sorrowful." This verse is saying, "Don't bring pain or distress to the Holy Spirit of God."

Before identifying what makes the Holy Spirit sad and sorrowful, I want to pick up where we left off in Ephesians 4:

> With the Lord's authority I say this: Live no longer as the Gentiles do, for they are hopelessly confused. Their minds are full of darkness; they wander far from the life God gives because they have closed their minds and hardened their hearts against him. They have no sense of shame. They live for lustful pleasure and eagerly practice every kind of impurity. (verses 17–19 NLT)

When a person truly meets Christ, changes take place in his or her life. On the other hand, if changes do not take place in a person's life, I have to question whether he or she has truly met Jesus Christ. The outward may be without the inward, but the inward is never without the outward. In other words, it is possible to put on a show and pretend to be a Christian and say the same things that Christians say. People who do this might be fooling others, but they are never fooling God. You can have the outward but not have the inward.

However, the inward is never without the outward. If you really have been transformed by Jesus, there will be outward signs of it. There will be results, or the fruit of the Spirit, as the Bible calls it. Your perspective will change. Your attitudes will change. Your outlook will change. Your worldview will change.

The New Testament speaks of the fact that when we become Christians, we receive a new mind, a new heart, new power, new knowledge, new love, new desires, and new citizenship. Paul summed it up perfectly when he wrote, "Anyone who belongs to Christ has become a new person. The old life is gone; a new life has begun!" (2 Corinthians 5:17 NLT). I love the way things look right after it rains. Even dirty cars look clean. Everything gets cleaned up. The streets look good. Everything is fresh and shiny in a way. The same is true when Christ comes into a person's life. There is a change.

Paul was saying to the believers in Ephesus, "You are new people." He told them, "Live no longer as the Gentiles do, for they are hopelessly confused" (verse 17 NLT). When we read the word *Gentile*, it may not mean a lot to us. But we could just as easily substitute the word *nonbeliever* in verse 17. Paul was writing primarily to a Jewish mind-set. When Jews speak of Gentiles, they are speaking of nonbelievers.

"Don't think like nonbelievers," Paul was saying. Why? Because "they are hopelessly confused." Another way to translate *confused* would be "empty-headed." It's empty thinking.

In Romans 12, Paul also said that we are to dedicate ourselves to the Lord and not be conformed to this world. As one translation puts it, "Don't let the world around you squeeze you into its own mould, but let God re-mould your minds from within, so that you may prove in practice that the plan of God for you is good, meets all his demands and moves towards the goal of true maturity" (verse 2 ph). Today it seems we've never had more knowledge and, at the same time, less wisdom. We can pull out our smartphones and do a search on just about anything we want. It's pretty amazing what we can pull up. (By the way, just because something is on the Internet doesn't mean it's true. Some people don't seem to know that.) We have this vast knowledge, but there is no depth and wisdom to go with it. We know so much, yet we understand so little.

It is said that nature abhors a vacuum. Whenever there is a vacuum, something will rush in to fill it. Paul said these empty minds are filled with darkness: "Their minds are full of darkness; they wander far from the life God gives because they have closed their minds and hardened their hearts against him. They have no sense of shame. They live for lustful pleasure and eagerly practice every kind of impurity" (Ephesians 4:18–19 NLT). If that was true then, how much more is it true today? Have we forgotten how to blush? The expressions people use today and the things they discuss so freely on television and in open forms would have shocked people even twenty or thirty years ago. Our culture is not unlike the one Isaiah described when he said, "Woe to those who call evil good and good evil, who put darkness for light and light for darkness" (Isaiah 5:20 NIV). Everything is upside down in American culture right now. Things are being applauded that should be criticized, and things are being criticized that should be applauded. It seems as though almost everything is out of sync.

That is how it was in the first century as well.

The phrase *lustful pleasure* Paul used in Ephesians 4:19 means "the absence of all moral restraint." Some people have no moral restraint. They chase after sin, almost as if to say, "What can I do next? How much deeper can I go?" They delve into all kinds of perversion. Paul was saying that is not how a Christian should live.

SINS AGAINST THE HOLY SPIRIT

As I said earlier, the Holy Spirit is the third person of the Trinity: Father, Son, and Holy Spirit. The Scriptures point out certain sins that can be committed against the Holy Spirit in particular.

For example, in Acts 5, we learn that people can lie to the Holy Spirit. That was the sin of Ananias and Sapphira. They pretended to give a certain amount of money to the church they actually hadn't given. They were putting on a show. They were hypocrites.

Sometimes people say they wish they could see more miracles today like we read about in the book of Acts. We should be thankful that God isn't doing some of these miracles today. Ananias and Sapphira were struck dead for their deception. If God dealt with the church today like He dealt with the church of the first century, in the case of Ananias and Sapphira, as Chuck Swindoll once said, "Every church would need a full-time undertaker on staff and a morgue in the basement." People would be dropping dead in church left and right. Thank God that He isn't dealing with us that way.

Another sin that can be committed against the Holy Spirit— and this would be committed by a believer—is quenching the Spirit. We can quench the Holy Spirit when God leads us to do something and we effectively say no. Maybe you suddenly feel prompted to go share Christ with a certain person or to read your Bible or to pray about something. When you say no, that is quenching the Spirit. And it's a sin.

Then there is resisting the Spirit. When Stephen preached to the Sanhedrin, the religious leaders of the day, he gave a wonderful overview of the history of Israel. Then he concluded with these words: "You stiff-necked people! Your hearts and ears are still uncircumcised. You are just like your ancestors:

You always *resist* the Holy Spirit!" (Acts 7:51 NIV). Of course, they stoned him. But the word Stephen used for *resist* conveys the idea of knowing that something is true and still choosing to resist it.

Not only can we lie to and resist the Holy Spirit, but we can insult Him. Hebrews 10:29 says, "Just think how much worse the punishment will be for those who have trampled on the Son of God, and have treated the blood of the covenant, which made us holy, as if it were common and unholy, and have *insulted and disdained the Holy Spirit* who brings God's mercy to us" (NLT). There's no question about it: we do not want to enrage the Spirit or insult the Spirit. But we can do this by rejecting the work of the Spirit.

Jesus said of the Holy Spirit, "And when He has come, He will convict the world of sin, and of righteousness, and of judgment" (John 16:8). The Holy Spirit has come to show us our need for Jesus. The way we insult Him is by resisting and rejecting His work. That can ultimately lead to the unforgivable sin: the blasphemy of the Holy Spirit.

Sometimes people will tell me they think they've blasphemed the Holy Spirit.

"Why do you think that?" I'll ask.

"I don't *feel* God right now," they tell me. "Maybe last night when I was sleeping, I just blasphemed Him. Or, maybe when I was a nonbeliever and cursed everyone and everything, maybe I cursed the Holy Spirit too."

First of all, they are asking about it with concern. And anyone who is concerned about this hasn't blasphemed the Holy Spirit. People who have actually blasphemed the Holy Spirit could care less about God. They could care less about church. They could care less about the Bible. In fact, they might go out of their way to mock Christians, to mock God, and to fight with God. I don't know when it happens in a person's life, but there is a point of no return. That is the blasphemy of the Holy Spirit.

Those are specific sins against the Spirit. Now let's look at what makes the Holy Spirit sad and sorrowful.

WHAT GRIEVES THE HOLY SPIRIT?

Verses 29–32 of Ephesians 4 tell us,

> Don't use foul or abusive language. Let everything you say be good and helpful, so that your words will be an encouragement to those who hear them. And do not bring sorrow to God's Holy Spirit by the way you live. Remember, he has identified you as his own, guaranteeing that you will be saved on the day of redemption. Get rid of all bitterness, rage, anger, harsh words, and slander, as well as all types of evil behavior. Instead, be kind to each other, tenderhearted, forgiving one another, just as God through Christ has forgiven you. (NLT)

Foul and Abusive Language

Foul and abusive language make the Holy Spirit sad. The terms Paul used here convey the idea of something being rotten. This includes obscene language, as well as taking the Lord's name in vain, profanity, dirty stories, vulgarity, and double entendres. This grieves God's Spirit. It makes God's Spirit sad. Don't let foul and abusive language be a part of your life.

Bitterness

Bitterness makes the Holy Spirit sad and sorrowful. The word *bitterness* refers here to an embittered and resentful spirit that refuses to be reconciled. I think some people actually like to be bitter. They are always mad about something. When one problem resolves itself, they have someone else to be mad at or something else that irritates them. It's as though they have a perpetual storm cloud over their heads. They find themselves usually dining alone, because no one wants to be around a person like this. When their table is ready, the hostess says, "Bitter, party of one?"

I have also found that bitter people can't keep it to themselves. They like to spread it around. That is why Hebrews 12:15 warns about a root of bitterness springing up and defiling many. Get rid of bitterness. If you don't, then here is what will happen next.

Anger and Rage

Paul wrote, "Get rid of all bitterness, rage, anger . . ." (verse 31). The word *rage* speaks of people who are easily angered. They are always raising their voices. You disagree with them, and it escalates in two seconds. This is called rage.

Sadly, some people live in environments like this. That is pretty much the story of my childhood for the first seventeen years. I lived with an alcoholic who screamed and yelled every night. There wasn't a time I went to bed when it was quiet and peaceful, except during the time I lived with my grandparents or in military school.

Don't let that be true of your home. Little eyes are watching. Little ears are listening. Think of your children. Think of the impact these things have on them. If you have a disagreement with your spouse (and you're going to disagree when you're married), never fight in front of your children. Never ask them to take sides in a disagreement. Go work it out with your spouse. Don't do it in front of the kids.

Slander

Slander is speaking evil of others. Some people love to slander. They will compliment you to your face and then stab you in the back. Sometimes they even will pretend to be concerned to get information out of you. Then they'll turn it around and give it a little twist, using it against you. They may do it on social media or in other ways. Sadly, this is the kind of culture we're living in now. People can hide behind a computer screen and say things in cyberspace they would never say to your face. Don't be that person.

That person who has wronged or offended you may deserve your unforgiveness, but you deserve even worse, and so do I. Paul tells us, "Be kind to each other, tenderhearted, forgiving one another, just as God through Christ has forgiven you" (verse 32).

God says, "Vengeance is Mine, I will repay" (Romans 12:19).

Augustine reportedly had this motto displayed on his dining-room wall: "He who speaks an evil word of an absent man or woman is not welcome at this table."[1]

That would be a great motto for us all to abide by. Let's be tenderhearted. Let's be forgiving of one another.

WHO WE ARE

Now let's shift gear to chapter 5 of Ephesians, where we'll learn more about how to walk as Christians:

> Therefore be imitators of God as dear children.
> And walk in love, as Christ also has loved us and
> given Himself for us, an offering and a sacrifice to
> God for a sweet-smelling aroma.

> But fornication and all uncleanness or covet-
> ousness, let it not even be named among you,
> as is fitting for saints; neither filthiness, nor
> foolish talking, nor coarse jesting, which are
> not fitting, but rather giving of thanks. For this
> you know, that no fornicator, unclean person,
> nor covetous man, who is an idolater, has any
> inheritance in the kingdom of Christ and God.
> (verses 1–5)

Before Paul tells us how to live, he begins by telling us who we are: "Therefore be imitators of God as dear children" (verse 1). I want you to think about this for a moment before we look at what we should and shouldn't do.

Did you know that you are precious and dear to God? We already have discovered in Ephesians that we have been made "accepted in the beloved" (1:6). That means God accepts you. He has forgiven you. And, of course, He loves you.

Jesus said to the Father, "I have given them the glory you gave me, so they may be one as we are one. I am in them and you are in me. May they experience such perfect unity that the world will know that you sent me and that you love them *as much as you love me*" (John 17:22–23 NLT, emphasis added). Did you notice what Jesus said? If you've missed everything else I've written here, don't miss this point: the Father loves you and me as much as He loves Jesus Christ. That is amazing.

What did we do to merit this?

Absolutely nothing.

Jesus died on the cross. He spilled His blood for us. He made us accepted in the beloved. Because of this new relationship we have with God through Christ, God looks at us with a smile on His face and love in His heart. He loves us as much as He loves

His own Son. If Jesus had not personally said it, I wouldn't have believed it. But it's true.

In light of that fact, how does God want us to live?

HOW SHOULD WE LIVE?

Stay Away from Immorality

First, we should steer clear of immorality. Verse 3 says, "But among you there must not be even a hint of sexual immorality" (NIV). Why would Paul bring this up with these believers?

Ephesus was a wicked city, as I've pointed out. In fact, it was renowned for its wickedness. It was the capital of the Roman province of Asia and a busy commercial port, making it a very wealthy and affluent area.

It also was the headquarters of the cult of the goddess Diana (or Artemis). Thousands of prostitutes worked for the Temple of Artemis. They would go out and find men whom they would bring back to the temple, and engage in sexual acts with them. This was in exchange for offering worship to this false goddess. Theirs was a sex-obsessed culture. And it goes without saying that Ephesus was not unlike our culture today. As Christians, we are to stay away from immorality.

The word Paul used in verse 3 for *immorality* refers to pre-marital sex, extramarital sex, and homosexual sex. It refers to all sex outside of marriage.

God created sex. And sex can be very good. But its only place is in a marriage between a man and a woman. Any other circumstances in which sex takes place never will be blessed by God.

Think how different our nation would be if we obeyed the commandment "You shall not commit adultery" (Exodus 20:14 niv). Think of the number of children who are born out of wedlock today without a family structure. Often, the cycle repeats itself again and again, all because we completely disregard what God says. That should not be true of a Christian.

Someone might say, "Oh, come on! Relax a little bit! Why is it so bad for unmarried people to have sex, as long as they are two consenting adults? Why did God lay down a law like this? Doesn't He know that we have raging hormones? Is He out to spoil all of our fun?"

What if we used the same rationale for driving? Imagine what would happen if we said, "Why do we have to stop at lights? Why can't we just drive wherever we want? The traffic is backing up. The oncoming lane is open. Why can't I just leave my lane and go around everyone?"

Well, technically, you can. But you might have a head-on collision. You might die. Other people might die. Those lanes are there for your own protection. Those traffic lights are there for your good. They are there to protect you.

In the same way, God gives us His commandments for the same reason. They are not for the purpose of making our lives miserable but to keep us safe. God has given us the absolutes of the Scriptures to protect us.

Watch Your Language

Again, in chapter 5, Paul addresses the way we speak: "Nor should there be obscenity, foolish talk or coarse joking, which are out of place, but rather thanksgiving" (verse 4 niv). We've already covered this earlier, but, in essence, don't tell dirty jokes. Stay away from filthy language. These things should not characterize a follower of Jesus Christ.

James said of the tongue, "And among all the parts of the body, the tongue is a flame of fire. It is a whole world of wickedness, corrupting your entire body. It can set your whole life on fire, for it is set on fire by hell itself" (James 3:6 NLT).

Don't Covet

Lastly, don't covet. Paul wrote, "For of this you can be sure: No immoral, impure or greedy person—such a person is an idolater—has any inheritance in the kingdom of Christ and of God" (verse 5 NIV).

"Well," you might say, "I don't think I've committed this sin. I have never coveted."

The problem is that many of us don't know what coveting really is. Yet it's such a serious issue that it made God's Top Ten list, the Ten Commandments.

Coveting means to eagerly desire something that belongs to someone else and to set your heart on it. Another way to translate it would be "to pant after something." It's like an animal panting after something it sees and wants.

We can be that way as well. That is why the Ten Commandments say, "You must not covet your neighbor's house. You must not covet your neighbor's wife, male or female servant, ox or donkey, or anything else that belongs to your neighbor" (Exodus 20:17 NLT). This is how coveting works: the eyes see it, the mind admires it, and the will goes over to it. But then the body moves in to possess it.

Let's say, for example, that your neighbor pulled into his driveway in a brand-new car. You check it out and think, *That is a nice car.* The next day, you go to the same dealership, and later that day, you pull into your driveway with the same color, make, and model as your neighbor's new car. That may be copying, but it isn't coveting. And it isn't a sin.

Coveting is different. If you said to your neighbor, "Your new car is really cool. I would love to see the inside. May I sit in it?"

"Go ahead," your neighbor says. "Sit in it."

"Wow, I love that new car smell! Do you mind if I turn this bad boy over?"

"Sure! Go ahead."

"Would you care if I took it around the block?"

"Go ahead."

But then you never come back with your neighbor's car. That is coveting. (And it's also grand theft auto.) The point is, the car doesn't belong to you. You took it from someone else. That is coveting.

Coveting has ruined many people because they have wanted something so badly, they were willing to give up anything to get it.

One example of this is Judas Iscariot. He was handpicked by Jesus Christ. He heard the Sermon on the Mount with his own ears. He saw Lazarus raised from the dead and Jesus walk on water. He was with Jesus in the Upper Room as Jesus broke the bread and distributed the cup. Judas saw it all. And then he sold out Jesus for thirty pieces of silver—payment that he ended up throwing on the ground and not even wanting. He was so greedy for what the world had to offer that it became more important to him than God.

There are people like that today. This is why the Bible says, "The love of money is a root of all kinds of evil, for which some have strayed from the faith in their greediness, and pierced themselves through with many sorrows" (1 Timothy 6:10).

That verse is often misquoted to say that money is the root of all evil. But the Bible doesn't say that. Money isn't the root of all evil. The *love of* money is the root of all evil, the Bible says.

You see, you can have a lot of money yet not *love* money. On the other hand, you can have very little money yet love money. It is not about how much is in your bank account; it is about what is going on in your heart. Someone can be obsessed with something to the point they will make any sacrifice to get it—and they leave God out of the picture. They end up selling out like Judas did.

Maybe as you've read this chapter you realize you've done some things that grieve the Holy Spirit. Maybe you're stuck in some of those sinful habits right now. You might even be thinking, *How did I get here? I can't believe this. It makes me sick to my stomach.*

The good news is that God can make things new again. Jesus says, "Come to Me, all you who labor and are heavy laden, and I will give you rest" (Matthew 11:28).

He can change your life if you will come to Him and say, "All right, Lord, this is a mess. I've gone after the wrong things. I've made the wrong decisions. Now I'm reaping the consequences."

God loved you so much that He sent His only Son, Jesus Christ, to go to the cross, die in your place, and then rise from the dead three days later. Jesus paid for your sins, and He will forgive you of your sins if you will turn from them and start following Him.

PART 2

LOVE

11

THE ULTIMATE AUTHORITY ON MARRIAGE AND SINGLENESS

Carefully determine what pleases the Lord. (Ephesians 5:10 NLT)

A husband and wife were celebrating their twenty-fifth wedding anniversary. The husband took his wife by the hand, and in front of their family and friends, announced that after twenty-five years of wedded bliss, he was giving her a trip to China.

"China! I've always wanted to go to China!" she exclaimed. "But if that is what you're doing for our twenty-fifth anniversary, then what will you do for our fiftieth?"

"That is when I'll be picking you up."

It has been said that marriage is like a three-ring circus: engagement ring, wedding ring, and suffering.

But does it have to be that way? Can a man and a woman fall in love, stay in love, get married, and live happily ever after?

I don't know about happily ever after. But how about happily *even* after? I believe that is possible.

Of course, there are a lot of threats against marriage today. The divorce rate in the United States is roughly 50 percent. However, that rises with second marriages, where it becomes 60 percent. And then, for third marriages, it rises even higher . . . to 73 percent. The problem is that people aren't doing it God's way.

We cannot look to this culture or to Hollywood for cues on how to have a successful relationship. (People in Hollywood can't seem to keep a relationship together for five months, much less a lifetime.) We need to look at what the Bible says about marriage. We want to do it God's way.

BUILD ON THE RIGHT FOUNDATION

Every marriage will be tested. Every marriage will be tried. Every marriage will be hit by storms.

The hardest thing my wife Cathe and I ever have had to face in our marriage was the death of our son Christopher in 2008. I am aware that some marriages have fallen apart when a child dies. It's a devastating thing to happen in a marriage. The reason Cathe and I were able to get through it, and continue to get through it, is because we have built our relationship on Jesus Christ. That is what sustained us and continues to sustain us. So does the hope that we will see our son again in Heaven.

Jesus used this analogy in His conclusion of the Sermon on the Mount:

> "Therefore everyone who hears these words of
> mine and puts them into practice is like a wise
> man who built his house on the rock. The rain
> came down, the streams rose, and the winds blew
> and beat against that house; yet it did not fall,
> because it had its foundation on the rock. But

everyone who hears these words of mine and does not put them into practice is like a foolish man who built his house on sand. The rain came down, the streams rose, and the winds blew and beat against that house, and it fell with a great crash." (Matthew 7:24–27 NIV)

That is a perfect picture of the family. They are building on a foundation. If a couple is building their marriage on the shifting sands of emotions and fluctuating feelings, it will collapse.

I have never understood why people build elaborate sand castles. It is only a matter of time until a wave washes them away or an aggressive little four-year-old boy comes and stomps on it, enjoying every moment.

A lot of people build their marriage on emotions or on sexual excitement. They don't understand that marriage is more than that. It must deepen beyond those things.

If you're married, here is my question for you: Is your marriage on the Rock, or is it on the rocks? If you build it on Jesus Christ, it will stand the test of time.

The storms *will* come to every relationship. Temptations will come. Hardships will come. Money issues will come. That is why a marriage has to be built on a proper foundation. That is why a husband and wife must have a commitment to do what the Bible says.

You may not know this about me, but I've been married to five different women. All of them were named Cathe, and all of them spell their name the same way. My point is the Cathe I married at age eighteen isn't the same Cathe I was married to at age thirty. The Cathe I was married to at age thirty is not the same Cathe I was married to at age forty. I'm going to stop there.

Cathe has changed over the years. *I* have changed over the years. I can say—and I wouldn't say this if it weren't true—that it gets better and better if we do it God's way.

When life is over, three things will bubble to the top of what really matters in life: faith, family, and at a distant third, friends.

When I talk to people who have come to the end of their lives, they are aware of the fact they should have been closer to God and how they should have spent more time in church, more time studying the Scriptures, and more time walking closely with the Lord.

Always a close second to that is family. They have regrets. They have regrets about the way they treated their spouse or their children.

One of the glorious things God gave to Cathe and me as a gift was that we had a fantastic relationship with our son when he was unexpectedly called home to Heaven. We didn't look back on our relationship with him with regrets.

On your deathbed, you are not going to think about how much stuff you own. It won't matter. As I have often said, you have never seen a hearse pulling a U-Haul trailer. You will leave it all. Your only concern will be to whom you will leave it.

On your deathbed, you will be thinking about God, and you will be thinking about family.

Instead of waiting until your deathbed, instead of waiting until you have a life filled with regrets, why not work on it now? Why not get it right so that you can have a strong and flourishing marriage now?

In far too many marriages, divorce is considered as an option—and in some instances only after a few days. Recent surveys have revealed that as many as two-thirds of those inter-viewed who identified themselves as Christians thought that divorce was a reasonable solution to a problem marriage.

It isn't.

Wedlock should be a padlock. If your marriage is miserable, the fault does not lie with the institution; it lies with the partici-pants.

People get into a cycle of selfishness they can't seem to break out of. Don't let that happen to you. Strong marriages don't come about by accident. It is not unlike your relationship with Christ. Show me someone who is growing spiritually, and I will show you someone who applies himself every single day. It has been said that the Christian life is like a greased pole: you are either climbing or slipping.

The same is true of marriage. The moment you stop pro-gressing, you begin the process of regressing. You must tend to, nurture, and care for your spouse and your family.

But we need God's help to do that. Probably one of the most definitive passages on this topic is Ephesians 5, where we are told how to have a strong and lasting marriage and how to do it God's way.

PRINCIPLES FOR A STRONG MARRIAGE

Before we get into God's specific words to husbands and wives, let's look at the introductory statements of this chapter, which apply to marriage:

For the light makes everything visible. This is why it is said,

"Awake,

O sleeper, rise up from the dead,

and Christ will give you light."

So be careful how you live. Don't live like fools, but like those who are wise. Make the most of every opportunity in these evil days. Don't act thoughtlessly, but understand what the Lord wants you to do. Don't be drunk with wine, because that will ruin your life. Instead, be filled with the Holy Spirit, singing psalms and hymns and spiritual songs among yourselves, and making music to the Lord in your hearts. And give thanks for everything to God the Father in the name of our Lord Jesus Christ.

And further, submit to one another out of reverence for Christ (Ephesians 5:13–21 NLT).

This passage provides us with several takeaway truths for a strong marriage.

Shine the Light of God's Word

Verse 13 tells us, "The light makes everything visible" (NLT). If you want a successful marriage, then shine the light of God's Word on it.

Have you ever lost something in your car? I lose things in the black interior in my car. I've lost burritos that I haven't seen for months. When you can't find something, you turn on the light.

It reminds me of a story I heard about a drunk man who was searching for his wallet under a streetlight. Someone asked him, "Did you lose your wallet here?"

He said, "No, I lost it down the street, but there is no street-light there."

It does no good to search for something if you go to the wrong place. Sometimes people who have marital problems will go to counseling. But my question is, what kind of counseling? Are they getting biblical counseling? We need scriptural counseling so that we're shining the light of God's Word on our marriages.

Psalm 1 says, "Blessed is the man who walks not in the counsel of the ungodly, nor stands in the path of sinners, nor sits in the seat of the scornful; but his delight is in the law of the Lord, and in His law he meditates day and night" (verses 1–2).

We need to look at what the Bible says to husbands and wives.

When someone comes to me for marital counseling, often I will ask a series of questions. The first question I ask is, "Are you a Christian?"

Usually, they'll say, "Of course. We love the Lord."

Then I'll ask, "Do you believe the Bible is the Word of God?"

"Oh yes, we love the Word of God."

My next question is, "Are you willing to do what the Bible says, even if you find it difficult?"

At this point, they know they're in trouble. They realize I'm about to tell them what the Bible says, and I'm about to ask them whether they're doing what it says.

People have asked me, "What if you don't agree with what the Bible says?"

If you don't agree with what the Bible says, then change your opinion, because you are wrong. The Bible is right. It's as simple as that.

If you're having problems in your marriage, you must admit that you have strayed from God's plan. If you're a husband, admit that you have not loved your wife as you ought to. If you're a wife, admit that perhaps you have not been the wife you should be.

Every husband, myself included, could love his wife more. And every wife could love her husband more.

Shine the light of God's Word on your marriage (and on everything else, for that matter).

Wake Up

Ephesians 5:14 says, "Awake, you who sleep" (NLT). You can't put your relationship with Christ on cruise control and expect it to go well. You have to be alert and aware, paying careful attention to the relationship you are in. The moment you neglect your spiritual life, you will falter. You can't live on what has happened in the past as a follower of Jesus.

The same is true for marriage. Wake up to the fact that our culture and this world system is not for marriage and family. Our Supreme Court now determines what they think marriage is. But God already has told us what it is in His Word. Our culture today does not value marriage. When I was growing up, there were sitcoms like *Father Knows Best*, *Leave It to Beaver*, *My Three Sons*, and *The Donna Reed Show*. Almost all of those shows featured a husband and a wife together. The father was wise and understanding. The mother was caring and nurturing. I understand these were only television shows. But there was a sense that the family is good, that a husband and wife together are good, and that a father and mother raising a child is good.

But not anymore. Today if you were to sum up what a father is like based on how they are portrayed in most sitcoms, you would say he is a complete idiot. Society doesn't value the family. Immorality is presented in an attractive way.

Let's wake from spiritual lethargy. Let's wake up to the fact that our culture does not support the family. The sooner we recognize that, the better.

Walk Carefully

Paul then writes, "See then that you walk circumspectly, not as fools but as wise" (Ephesians 5:15). The word *circumspectly* in this verse has the basic meaning of that which is accurate and exact. It carries the idea of looking, examining, and investigating something with great care.

The devil is in the details, as they say. Read the fine print. Understand what you are committing yourself to. Get it right.

In the same way, as we read the Bible, we know what has been approved by God. Study it carefully. Look at the details of it. It tells you how to do things. Walk carefully.

To walk *circumspectly* also carries the idea of alertness. That means going into your marriage saying that failure is not an option. It means saying, "We're going to make this marriage work."

Winston Churchill once said that "wars are not won by evacuation." The same principle applies to marriage.

When Cathe and I got married, I never considered anything close to divorce. That never was an option. And by God's grace, we have been married for forty-two years now. We are thankful for that.

Use Your Time Wisely

Paul continues, "Redeeming the time, because the days are evil" (Ephesians 5:16). The word *redeem* means to make the most of your time. Use your time wisely. Years ago, the prophet Isaiah came to see King Hezekiah and told him, "Put your house in order, because you are going to die" (2 Kings 20:1 NIV).

Is your house in order? Get your life right with God. Do what you can to strengthen your marriage.

Be Filled with the Holy Spirit

To have a successful marriage, you must be filled with the Holy Spirit. And to have a successful Christian life, you must be filled with the Holy Spirit. Paul goes on to say in Ephesians 5, "And do not be drunk with wine, in which is dissipation; but be filled with the Spirit" (verse 18). In Greek, this is in the imperative mode, meaning it's a command. To fail to obey this will cut off your power supply, the Holy Spirit.

Years ago, we had a workday at our church in Riverside. I am not a handyman (just ask my wife), but I went to help anyway. We were cleaning up trash, painting, and trimming hedges. I noticed an electric trimmer sitting on top of a hedge, plugged in and ready to go.

I thought, *That looks fun.* So I picked it up and started working on the hedge. Sure enough, it wasn't long before I sliced right through the cord. I looked this way and that way. Then I set the trimmer down and walked off. I was so embarrassed that I didn't want to tell anyone what had happened.

A friend of mine, Dennis, was up on the roof that day. Years later, he told me he had seen the whole thing.

We can do in life what I did at our church workday: we can cut our own power source.

We need the power of the Spirit. And the filling of the Holy Spirit will empower you to be the husband or wife God calls you to be.

Paul concludes these verses by saying, "And further, submit to one another out of reverence for Christ" (verse 21 NLT). If you are a Spirit-filled person, then you will be a submitting person. We don't like the word *submission*. We get really hung up on that word, thinking, *I don't submit to anyone.*

Yes, we do. When the police officer signals you to pull over, you'd better submit. When your boss says, "Come into my office," you'd better submit. When the teacher tells you to pay attention in class, you'd better submit.

We submit all day long. And so we should.

Note that Paul said, "Submit *to one another* out of reverence for Christ" (emphasis added). If you are truly Spirit-filled, then you will think of others more than yourself. The Spirit-filled husband puts the needs of his wife above his own. The Spirit-filled wife puts the needs of her husband above her own.

In a military sense, *submit* could be translated "to rank beneath" or "to rank under." It is not so much who is more important. It is not about superiority or inferiority. It is about the role of a husband and a wife. God has established roles in the marriage relationship.

If a woman goes into her marriage saying, "This guy is going to make me happy. He will meet all of my needs," she will have trouble. And if a man goes into the marriage saying, "This woman is going to make all of my dreams come true," he too will have problems.

Marriage is not so much about finding the right person as it is about *being* the right person. Be the best husband you can be. Be the best wife you can be.

Successful marriages require dependence on God and the application of biblical principles. Marriages unravel when these two things are not practiced; when there is no effort put into the marriage and there is no prayer put into it. Couples are disregarding what the Scripture says.

IRRECONCILABLE DIFFERENCES?

Having been a pastor for more than forty years, I have counseled a lot of couples. And I can say that most marriages I have seen fall apart didn't have to.

So many couples claim to have irreconcilable differences. The question I would ask them is, "What drew you to each other in the first place?"

More often than not, the answer is they were so different from each other. They discovered they complemented each other, even completed each other. But then a wide chasm develops. They think they can't even be in the same room with each other. They're convinced their differences are "irreconcilable."

I think they need to go back, embrace those distinctions, and say, "*Vive la différence!*"

You couldn't find any two people that are more different than Cathe and me. We've had "irreconcilable differences" for forty-two years. They are differences. And they are irreconcilable. She's neat. I'm messy. She's sometimes late. I'm usually early. She likes British television dramas. I like shoot 'em ups. Our differences are what drew us together. That is why we like to be with each other. That is why we love each other.

If you're having marital problems right now, and if, in your mind, your mate is the sole person responsible, then I already know that a great deal of the problem is with you. If you don't think you're playing a part in a marriage that is unraveling, then you're living in a fantasy world. Successful marriages are the result of a lot of hard work and a lot of effort.

And just as married people need God's power to be the husbands and wives God calls them to be, unmarried people need God's power as well.

A WORD TO SINGLES

God has a very unique plan for the single man or woman. Having said that, I don't want to imply that you are inferior or a second-class citizen if you are single. There are people who are called to be single for a lifetime. And there are many single people today who will be married in time. Studies have shown that nine out of ten people are married at some point in their lives. Which means that even if you may be single today, it's very likely the truths I have discussed in this chapter will matter to you at some point in your life.

I believe that if you're single and a follower of Jesus Christ, God specifically has chosen someone for you to marry (unless He has called you to remain single). I believe that he or she is just the right person and that you can start praying for this individual right now.

But I would also add this. When you are looking for the right person, don't identify an individual and say, "I love this person, but I'm going to change him [or her]."

Chances are that you won't. In fact—and I hate to break this to you—he or she might get worse. That person just may become a more exaggerated version of himself or herself, good or bad.

"But I will change this person," you might be saying.

No, you probably won't. Don't make that individual your little project. He is what he is. She is what she is. If you can't live with that, then don't go down that road.

When you're single, you often wish you were married. But there are married people today who would say, "If only I were single again, I know I would be happy."

The bottom line is there are advantages and disadvantages to being single. And, frankly, there are advantages and disadvantages to being married. Paul addressed this in 1 Corinthians 7:

> An unmarried man can spend his time doing the Lord's work and thinking how to please him. But a married man has to think about his earthly responsibilities and how to please his wife. His interests are divided. In the same way, a woman who is no longer married or has never been married can be devoted to the Lord and holy in body and in spirit. But a married woman has to think about her earthly responsibilities and how to please her husband. I am saying this for your benefit, not to place restrictions on you. I want you to do whatever will help you serve the Lord best, with as few distractions as possible. (verses 32–35 NLT)

Paul was saying that when you are married, you must consider your mate and how to please him or her. That isn't a criticism; it's a practical acknowledgment of reality. When you are married, you have to think about your husband. You have to think about your wife. They are a very important part of your life. That isn't to say it is a bad thing to be married. In fact, it is a very good thing to be married. Proverbs 18:22 says, "He who finds a wife finds what is good and receives favor from the lord" (NIV). But when you're single, you have mobility that you don't have when you're married—especially when you're married and have children. If you're single, you want to use that mobility to bring glory to God and do what you can for His kingdom while you can.

Whether married or single, you want to find contentment in the place you are right now. As Paul said, "I have learned in whatever state I am, to be content" (Philippians 4:11). We also read in Hebrews, "Let your conduct be without covetousness; be content with such things as you have. For He Himself has said, 'I will never leave you nor forsake you'" (13:5).

If you're single, don't think you're going to find total fulfillment in marriage. That comes first from your relationship with God. Start there. Find your contentment there, walking with Him.

I would also offer this warning: Don't be willing to go out with someone simply because he or she claims to be a Christian. Look for a godly man. Look for a godly woman. And as you wait on God to bring that person into your life, rely on the power of the Holy Spirit to help you resist sexual temptation and wait for marriage.

Some people seem to be shocked that after they look at pornography, their minds are filled with sexual thoughts. You don't feed lust; you starve it. When you feed your mind with that kind of junk, you will create a lot of trouble for yourself.

There is so much pressure on singles today to find out if you are compatible in every way, including sexually. They move in and live together in sort of a trial run. But there isn't a worse way to start a relationship than to live with a man or woman outside of marriage. Studies show that couples who live together before they are married have a far higher divorce rate than those who wait until they are married to be together.

If you are single, you need to wait on God's timing. You need to resist sexual temptation. God tells you, "No temptation has overtaken you except what is common to mankind. And God is faithful; he will not let you be tempted beyond what you can bear. But when you are tempted, he will also provide a way out so that you can endure it" (1 Corinthians 10:13 NIV). Whenever you are tempted, there is always a way out. Think of any temptation you have given in to. Was there a way out? Of course there was. Sometimes the way out was as simple as the door or the off button on the remote control. There is *always* a way out.

Sometimes the best way out of temptation is to be like Joseph when he was tempted by Potiphar's wife. She was far from subtle. She said, "Lie with me." In other words, "Have sex with me."

Joseph did what any clear-thinking, red-blooded young man would do under such circumstances. He ran like crazy. He said, "I'm out of here."

Sometimes it's as simple as that.

If you're single, God will give you the power to resist temptation. If you're married, God will give you the power to be the husband or wife He has called you to be.

POWER FOR LIVING

Have you ever been driving along in your car when your "idiot light" came on? By idiot light, I mean the little indicator that tells you it's time to refuel. I don't know about you, but I always put this off. I somehow think I will save more money if I wait until the last minute. And my wife runs on fumes. In her mind, that little red line for empty is merely a guideline. I've gotten into the car after she has driven it and proceeded straight to the gas station, praying the entire time that I would make it before I ran out of gas.

Just as we need to regularly refuel our cars to keep them going, we need to be refilled with the Spirit to keep going in the Christian life.

On the day of Pentecost, when the Holy Spirit was poured out upon the church (see Acts 2), it was a one-of-a-kind event, never to be repeated. We don't need another Pentecost any more than we need another Calvary.

But in Acts 4, we read about Peter being filled with the Holy Spirit as he spoke to the Sanhedrin (verse 8). We are also told that as Peter, John, and the church prayed, "they were all filled with the Holy Spirit and spoke the word of God boldly" (verse 31 NIV). Does this mean that every time we pray for the filling of the Holy Spirit, the room will shake?

No.

Does this mean that every time we pray for the empowering and filling of the Holy Spirit, we will have an emotional experience?

Again, no.

It helps to know what the word *filled* means. The Greek word used here is a fascinating one that can be translated multiple ways. A number of word pictures bring the meaning home. One conveys the idea of wind filling a sail and carrying a vessel along the surface of the water. That is what it's like to be filled with the Spirit. He gives us the power to do what He calls us to do.

When you're filled with the Holy Spirit, God's commandments are not a drudgery but a delight. You find yourself wanting to obey God, not because you have to but because you want to. The Holy Spirit gives you that desire.

Another meaning of *filled* in the original language conveys the idea of permeation, as in salt permeating meat. In the first century, there wasn't refrigeration like we have today. When they wanted their meat to last awhile, they would rub salt into it, deeply permeating the meat and causing it to last longer.

Thus, being filled with the Spirit speaks of the Holy Spirit permeating your entire life, not just part of it. God wants to permeate the lives of His children, including what we say, what we think, and what we do. He wants to influence us in our marriages, in our singleness, in our work, and in our worldview.

Finally, the word *filled* communicates the idea of being under the control of something. Have you ever been really scared? You came under the control of fear. Have you ever been extremely sad to the point that you were under the control of grief? That is the idea here. Being filled with the Spirit is coming under the Holy Spirit's control.

To put it all together, to be filled with the Spirit is to be carried along, permeated by, and under the control of the Holy Spirit. We fill ourselves with God's Word, and His thoughts become our thoughts. His standards become our standards. His will becomes our will.

To be filled with the Spirit is to walk thought by thought, decision by decision, under the Holy Spirit's control and leading.

You need the power of the Holy Spirit. That's why it's a good idea to pray every day, "Lord, fill me with the Holy Spirit."

He will fill you, and then He will refill you and fill you again.

If you want to be the best husband or the best wife you can be, if you want to be the best single person you can be, if you want to be the best Christian you can be, then you need to be filled with the Holy Spirit.

12

GOD'S PLAN FOR SEX AND MARRIAGE

"For this reason a man shall leave his father and mother and
be joined to his wife, and the two shall become one flesh."
(Ephesians 5:31)

I like to surf. But I usually do it only when I'm in Hawaii, when
I'm in the mood, and when it's the perfect-sized wave. Here in
California, the water is always so cold. Whenever I do go into the
ocean in California, I realize there is only one way to do it: all at
once.

My wife, however, doesn't think that is the way to go.

I'll tell her, "Cathe, just immerse yourself." The best way is
to just take the leap.

The same is true of marriage. It's a total commitment.

I read an interesting article the other day about the state of
marriage in the United States. It cited a 2014 survey of Millenni-
als in which 43 percent said they "would support a 'beta' marriage model: testing relationships for two years before deciding
to commit or dissolve." And 36 percent of them liked the idea
of a so-called real estate marriage model where "couples would
commit to a set period of time . . . and at the end have to renego-
tiate if they wanted to remain married."[1]

You commit to a marriage. There is no safety net. There is no backup plan. There is no "beta" or "real estate" model. That is why you want to take your time before you take the leap.

It has been said, "Keep your eyes wide open before marriage and half shut afterward."

Yet many times people do the opposite. Their eyes are half shut before marriage, and afterward they wonder what they have gotten themselves into.

If you're single, take your time in finding the right person. The Bible says, "Many waters cannot quench love, nor can the floods drown it" (Song of Solomon 8:7). It also says, "Love is patient" (1 Corinthians 13:4 NIV). Don't tell me you're in love with someone and want to get married immediately. Just slow down. You want to have a marriage that will last for a lifetime.

I am amazed at how people will obsess about their wedding and think very little of their marriage. Or, they will spend all of their time thinking about their house and never give any thought to the home.

I wish that we as Christians could strike the very word *divorce* from our vocabularies. As I said earlier, wedlock should be a padlock. If you aren't willing to make that commitment, then do everyone a favor and just stay single.

Better yet, do marriage God's way. If you've seen someone who has a happy marriage and fulfilling marriage, it did not happen by accident. If a marriage is strong and thriving, it is because two people have done their part. The man has done his part, and the woman has done hers.

I find it interesting that God uses marriage as a picture of His love for us:

Husbands, love your wives, just as Christ loved the church and gave himself up for her to make her holy, cleansing her by the washing with water through the word, and to present her to himself as a radiant church, without stain or wrinkle or any other blemish, but holy and blameless. In this same way, husbands ought to love their wives as their own bodies. He who loves his wife loves himself. After all, no one ever hated their own body, but they feed and care for their body, just as Christ does the church—for we are members of his body. (Ephesians 5:25–30 NIV)

God could have chosen a lot of comparisons. But here God is saying, "Okay, world, pay attention. Do you see how this Christian man loves his wife? That is how much I love the church. Do you see how this Christian wife loves her husband? That is how much my church loves Me. Look at this marriage as an example and a reflection of My love for humanity." He certainly loves each and every one of us.

That is why it is so devastating when Christian marriages fall apart.

God has given us the user's manual on marriage—and on every other subject, for that matter. I like the acronym BIBLE: Basic Instructions Before Leaving Earth. That is what the Bible is. Read it, and it will tell you how to do marriage the right way. Ignore it, and you'll do so at your own peril.

MARRIAGE IS GOD'S IDEA

In the book of Ephesians, we can learn about God's plan for a man and woman in marriage and how they can have a successful marriage. Paul quotes from Genesis 2, which is really where we see marriage introduced in the Bible: "For this reason a man shall leave his father and mother and be joined to his wife, and the two shall become one flesh" (Ephesians 5:31).

God placed Adam in the Garden of Eden. We may think of Eden as a fairy-talelike place, such as Camelot or Neverland or Atlantis. But Eden was a real place where real people were involved in real events.

Eden was more beautiful than anything you have ever seen or could even imagine. Think of the most wonderful places you have visited or have perhaps seen in a movie or photograph. Eden surpassed all of those. Eden was absolute perfection.

Adam had the coolest job ever in the Garden of Eden. His job was to discover the secrets of all that God placed in the garden. There was no danger. There was no threat to his life. There was no illness. Then, to make it even better, the Lord would show up every day, in the cool of the day, and Adam and the Lord would take a little walk together. How amazing that must have been. He could have asked the Lord about things he had seen that day and the discoveries he had made.

As beautiful as all of this was, however, something—or I should say someone—was missing. When we read the creation account in Genesis 1, we also find the phrase "and God saw that it was good." But then, in Genesis 2, God looked at Adam's loneliness and said it was *not* good: "It is not good that man should be alone; I will make him a helper comparable to him" (verse 18).

"A helper" could be literally translated, "someone who assists another to reach fulfillment." Another version puts it this way: "a helper suited to his needs" (TLB). God invented marriage. It was His idea, and we need to do it His way. To me, it's absurd that our Supreme Court has redefined what marriage should be. We know from the Bible what the definition is: A man and a woman in a commitment that should last for a lifetime.

We have built our very nation on marriage and the family. Our first president, George Washington, warned, "The smiles of Heaven can never be expected on a nation that disregards the eternal rules of order and right, which Heaven itself has ordained."[2]

A family can survive without a nation, but a nation cannot survive without the family. This is God's order. This is His plan. The institution of marriage has been tested by millions of people over centuries and in multiple cultures and has not only survived, but flourished.

Timothy Keller wrote, "Marriage did not evolve in the late Bronze Age as a way to determine property rights. At the climax of the Genesis account of creation we see God bringing a man and a woman together to unite them in marriage. The Bible begins with a wedding (of Adam and Eve) and ends in the book of Revelation with a wedding (of Christ and the church). Marriage is God's idea."[3]

LEAVE AND CLEAVE

Why did God bring the woman to the man? She would provide what was missing in his life. There are two words that can sum up what God's objective for marriage is: *leave* and *cleave*. These come from verse 24 of Genesis 2: "Therefore shall a man leave his father and his mother, and shall cleave unto his wife: and they shall be one flesh" (KJV). The word *cleave* in Hebrew means "to glue" or "to cling." It is leaving one thing and taking hold of another. It is loosening and securing. It is departing from and attaching to.

Leaving

If you want a successful and lasting marriage, it starts with *leaving*—leaving all other relationships, that is. The closest relationship outside of marriage is specified here, which is that of a son to his parents. It is necessary to leave your father and mother, then certainly all lesser ties need to be broken, changed, or left behind. When you are married, your primary responsibility is to your spouse, and then later to your children as well, if you have children. That is not to say that a young man should no longer honor his mother and father. But it is to say that a new relationship has begun that is more important than any other.

Leaving and cleaving also means that your best friend should be your husband or your wife. You can have other friendships, but your best friend needs to be your spouse. Sometimes marriages start that way but don't continue that way.

Malachi 2:14 is a key verse that emphasizes the importance of friendship between husband and wife: "The Lord has been witness between you and the wife of your youth, with whom you have dealt treacherously; yet she is your companion and your wife by covenant."

God says she is your *companion* and *wife*—not just your wife. She is your companion. The word *companion* means "one you are united with in thoughts, goals, plans, and efforts."

How well do you really know your husband or wife? What is his favorite color? What is her favorite kind of music? What is his favorite food? What is her favorite thing to do?

As I mentioned earlier, Cathe and I could not be any more opposite, including in what we like to do. But we always reach a little compromise. Sometimes I go her way. Sometimes she comes my way. The point is, you work those compromises out.

Husbands, if you are not tuned in to your wife, the Bible says it can actually hinder your prayer life: "Husbands, in the same way be considerate as you live with your wives, and treat them with respect as the weaker partner and as heirs with you of the gracious gift of life, so that nothing will hinder your prayers" (verse 7 NIV). The New King James Version puts it this way: "Dwell with them with understanding." The word *dwell* means "to be aligned to" or "give maintenance to." It isn't just a matter of living under the same roof.

You give maintenance to your house. You give maintenance to your body. You even give maintenance to your car. Do you give maintenance to your marriage?

Keep working at it. Keep maintaining it. Keep giving attention to it.

Notice to whom these words are directed:

> "For this reason *a man* shall leave his father and mother and be joined to his wife, and the two shall become one flesh." (Ephesians 5:31, emphasis added)

> "Husbands, likewise, dwell with them with understanding." (1 Peter 3:7)

> "Husbands, love your wives, just as Christ also loved the church and gave Himself for her." (Ephesians 5:25)

I believe if husbands would do their part, wives would respond in the right way. I think the reasons a lot of marriages aren't working today is that husbands are not the spiritual leaders they're supposed to be.

I thank God for Christian women. If Christian women didn't go to church one Sunday, we probably would collapse overnight.

So often in the Christian home it is the woman who takes the initiative. It is the woman who says, "Honey, get ready for church."

It is the woman who says, "Let's read a Bible story to the kids."

It is the woman who reminds the husband to pray.

It is the woman who reminds the husband they should be giving to the Lord.

It is the woman who is often the leader.

Thank God for the women who are using their influence. But the guys are supposed to lead. The husbands are supposed to take the initiative in the home. I believe that if we men did our part, it would change everything.

Again, Paul wrote to husbands, "Love your wives, just as Christ also loved the church and gave Himself for her" (Ephesians 5:25).

Why am I a Christian? Why are you a Christian? The Bible gives the answer: "We love Him because He first loved us" (1 John 4:19).

You love him because what? He first loved us.

Jesus Christ won me over with His love. I ran out of excuses. I believed in Him just like you did. I also believe that if a husband would be the man that God has called him to be, it would change everything. Becoming one flesh happens in a technical sense when you are pronounced husband and wife. But it is also a lifelong pursuit.

Cleaving

You leave, and then you cleave. What does it mean to cleave? The word *cleave* could be translated "to adhere to," "to stick," or "to be attached by some strong tie." It doesn't say you are stuck; it says you are to stick. There is a difference. In fact, the verb suggests a determined action.

There is nothing passive about the act of cleaving. It is like rock climbers (I think they're crazy, by the way). You see them clinging to the face of a cliff or a mountain, hanging on for dear life. That is the idea. That is what it is to cleave. You aren't stuck together; you're holding on to one another. There's a difference.

The New Testament term *cleave* could be translated "to cement together," "to stick like glue," or "to be welded together so the two cannot be separated without serious damage to both."

Have you ever used superglue? I have not been successful with that. I was putting a model together awhile back and got it on my thumb and another finger. I thought my fingers would be in the okay sign permanently. That is the idea of cleaving. You are adhere together.

One of the ways this cleaving is expressed is through sexual union. Some people think the Bible is somehow disapproving of sex. Nothing could be further from the truth. We sometimes forget that God created sex. It was God who told Adam and Eve to "be fruitful and multiply" (Genesis 1:28). Sex can be wonderful. It can be fulfilling. It can even be blessed if it is in its proper place. And the only place where sex can be fulfilling and blessed is in a marriage relationship.

God is very specific about this. Hebrews 13:4 says, "Marriage should be honored by all, and the marriage bed kept pure, for God will judge the adulterer and all the sexually immoral" (NIV). Imagine taking soil out of a garden, admiring it, and then walking inside and throwing it on white carpet. It was great in its proper place. But out of that proper place, it is no longer a thing of beauty.

The same is true of sex. It is great in marriage. But it is destructive outside of it. We were not designed for multiple sexual relationships. Casual sexual encounters are made to look harmless and fun in sitcoms. But in real life, there are far more serious and devastating consequences.

Think how different our nation would be if people would pay attention to the simple commandment "You shall not commit adultery" (Exodus 20:14), would wait until marriage to have sex, and would be faithful to their spouse for life. The United States would be a different place. You can trace almost every social ill in our country today to broken homes, and specifically to the absence of fathers. Studies bear this out.

Instead, our culture says, "Who needs the Bible? The Bible is outdated."

I remember watching a minister who was being interviewed on television, and the interviewer said, "Sir, don't you think it is time to bring the Bible kicking and screaming into the twenty-first century?"

I wanted to jump through that television screen and say, "No! It is time to bring our culture kicking and screaming back to the Bible, because that is why everything is going wrong today."

Sex was given by God to be enjoyed by two married people to enter into a state of oneness. But for many, it is like a recreational sport.

People will say, "Well, sex is natural. It should not be repressed. Why is it wrong to have sex with someone, even if you are not married to them? Hey, if they are two consenting adults, don't you think it's okay?"

God laid these standards down for our own good. It may not seem like it, but it really is for our own good.

Imagine, for example, that you are driving on the freeway and get behind someone who is going well below the speed limit in the fast lane. (They are usually driving a Prius.)

You say, "Why do I have to stay in this lane? I'm going to go into the oncoming lane and go around everything." (By the way, they actually do that in some countries.)

The problem is that if you pull into the oncoming lane, there might be a car coming your way that you don't see. You could have a head-on collision and kill yourself and someone else. Those lanes are there for your own protection.

It's the same with traffic lights. People run red lights all the time. They disregard the laws, and when they do, something bad often happens.

In the same way, God has given us His commandments and the truths of Scripture for our own protection. When a man and a woman come together, a unity takes place—a oneness. And this oneness happens even if you are not married. The Bible says, "And don't you realize that if a man joins himself to a prostitute, he becomes one body with her? For the Scriptures say, 'The two are united into one.' . . . Run from sexual sin! No other sin so clearly affects the body as this one does. For sexual immorality is a sin against your own body" (1 Corinthians 6:16, 18 NLT). This kind refutes the idea of the one-night stand and the assertion that it didn't mean anything; it was just sex. God gave sex for a special expression of love between a man and a woman who are committed to each other in marriage. It is not a toy; it is a gift from God.

"But it doesn't hurt anyone," someone might say.

Really? What about sexually transmitted diseases? What about AIDS? What about the innocent babies that have been slaughtered through abortion?

Life begins at conception, not at birth. Once that child is conceived, no matter how it happened, the child should be carried to term. If a woman doesn't want to raise the child, then she can put the little one up for adoption. I have talked with mothers who had abortions years ago and didn't think much of it then. Then, as time passes, they find themselves looking at children who are the same age as that child would have been, and they realize what they have done. It is a heavy weight to carry. Thank God for the forgiveness of Jesus Christ for a woman who has done this.

Extramarital sex does hurt people. It hurts a lot of people.

In marriage, there should be a sexual union, and it is not something you want to start holding back from your mate. Paul wrote in 1 Corinthians 7,

> But since sexual immorality is occurring, each
> man should have sexual relations with his own
> wife, and each woman with her own husband. The
> husband should fulfill his marital duty to his wife,
> and likewise the wife to her husband. The wife
> does not have authority over her own body but
> yields it to her husband. In the same way, the hus-

band does not have authority over his own body
but yields it to his wife. (verses 2–4 NIV)

When you are married, you want to meet the needs of your
mate.

You should periodically ask yourself, *Is there is any relationship or pursuit I'm currently involved in that could put distance
between me and my spouse?*

Sometimes it's a hobby. Sometimes it's work. Sometimes it's
a friendship. Is there something that is starting to stress out your
marriage?

If you find something starting to weaken the bond with your
spouse, that needs to go on the chopping block, or it needs to be
altered somehow. This comes from communication.

For example, if a wife says, "Honey, I think you're spending
way too much time doing that" or a husband says, "I'm not comfortable with you hanging out with him," then it's time to make a
change.

By the way, it's very problematic to have friendships with
the opposite sex when you're married. Let's be real here. Most
affairs happen between people who work closely together. You
have to be careful. It's a matter of constant communication
with your spouse. Communication is the lifeblood of the
relationship.

In one study where divorced people were asked why their
marriage failed, 86 percent cited deficient communication.
That is why husbands and wives need to learn how to
communicate.

They also need to learn how to argue. I've had couples come
to me and ask me to perform their wedding. I'll ask them how

long they have known each other. Then I'll ask them to tell me about their last argument.

"We've never had an argument."

"Really?"

"Oh no. We don't disagree about anything. We just love each other so much."

At that point, I'll tell them the meeting is over, and it's time for them to go have an argument.

Why would I say such a thing?

Because they will need to learn how to resolve conflict. In a marriage, they will need to know how to bend, how to compromise, how to resolve, and how to forgive.

Don't go into your marriage saying, "How can my spouse make me happy?"

Instead, go into your marriage saying, "How can I make my spouse happy?"

So often we are very selfish. We are together for a time, and then suddenly we think our marriage has sort of lost its spark.

I like this statement from C. S. Lewis about marriage:

> People get from books the idea that if you have married the right person you may expect to go on "being in love" forever. As a result, when they find they are not, they think this proves they have made a mistake and are entitled to a change—not realizing that, when they have changed, the glamour will presently go out of the new love just as it went out of the old one. In this department of life,

as in every other, thrills come at the beginning and do not last. . . . the dying away of the first thrill will be compensated for by a quieter more lasting kind of interest.[4]

Some couples, when they hit rough waters, say, "That's it. We're going to dissolve this marriage."

Not so fast. Hang in there. In a study that was done on couples who were having conflict but stayed together, two-thirds of the unhappily married couples who stayed together reported five years later that their marriages were very happy.

Most striking are long-term studies demonstrating that two-thirds of unhappy marriages will become happy within five years if the couple stays married and doesn't get divorced.

What God wants is for you to do what He told you to do. God wants you to be holy a whole lot more than He wants you to be happy.

Happiness never will come if we seek it outright. In fact, if you want to be an unhappy person, then dedicate your life to becoming a happy person. The best way to find happiness is by seeking the Lord.

While being married is incredible, it won't meet all the needs in your life. A husband or wife simply won't be able to fulfill everything inside you. Deep down inside, what you are looking for is God.

As Jesus told the woman at the well in Samaria, "Anyone who drinks this water will soon become thirsty again. But those who drink the water I give will never be thirsty again. It becomes a fresh, bubbling spring within them, giving them eternal life" (John 4:13–14 NLT).

Jesus was saying, "Here is your problem: You have been going to the well of marriage over and over again, and you are not satisfied. If you drink of that well, you will thirst again."

The same is true for us today. Some go to the well of sex looking for fulfillment. Others go to the well of drugs. Others go to the well of alcohol. Others go to the well of success. Others go to the well of material things. But Jesus says, "If you drink of the water that I give, you will never thirst again, because that water will well up from within."

That is what we need and want deep down inside. We want God. We want Jesus Christ. We were prewired that way.

WHAT ABOUT SAME-SEX ATTRACTION?

Then there is the question of same-sex attraction. If a guy says he isn't attracted to women, he's attracted to men, and if a woman says she isn't attracted to guys, she's attracted to women, does this mean they are gay?

According to our culture, the answer is a resounding yes.

But I disagree. The Bible doesn't teach that, and science doesn't support it. No fewer than eight major studies around the world have found that homosexuality is not a genetic condition.[5] Numerous, rigorous studies of identical twins have now made it impossible to argue there is a so-called gay gene. If homosexuality were inborn and predetermined, then when one identical twin is homosexual, the other would be as well. Researchers Dr. Peter Bearman, from Columbia University and Dr. Hannah Bruckner, from Yale, have concluded that environment determines your orientation.[6]

No one is born gay. However, we are born sinful. We are born with sinful tendencies. Some are attracted to some things, and others are attracted to other things. We have all had some of the strangest temptations knock on the doors of our imaginations. But the sin of temptation is not in the bait; it is in the bite.

The problem is when you take that idea and bring it into your thought processes and start running with it, start fantasizing about it, and ultimately, start acting on it. To be tempted is not a sin. We are born sinful.

I spoke with someone awhile back who was struggling with same-sex attraction. I said, "Here is the key: You can't act on these impulses. If you act on them, it's a sin."

The Bible says that homosexuality, along with a host of other things, is a sin:

Don't you realize that those who do wrong will not inherit the Kingdom of God? Don't fool yourselves. Those who indulge in sexual sin, or who worship idols, or commit adultery, or are male prostitutes, or practice homosexuality, or are thieves, or greedy people, or drunkards, or are abusive, or cheat people— none of these will inherit the Kingdom of God. (1 Corinthians 6:9–10 NLT)Here is the key: You don't respond to the temptation. At the same time, you don't define yourself by it either. You are defined by the grace of God, not by what tempts you. You don't have to give into those impulses.

I believe that a man or woman who is not attracted to members of the opposite sex should remain celibate. However, I do know people who have left a gay lifestyle and are now living a heterosexual lifestyle. They are happily married and have children. It does happen. The Bible says, "Therefore, if anyone is in Christ, he is a new creation; old things have passed away; behold, all things have become new" (2 Corinthians 5:17).

START AGAIN

We have all tried and failed on so many levels. Some have been in a sexually promiscuous situation and are living with the guilt. Some have had an abortion. Some have been unfaithful to their spouse. Here is the good news: God can forgive your sins if you ask for His forgiveness, and you can start over again.

Starting today, you can tend to your marriage, cultivate your marriage, and pay attention to your marriage. God can bless your marriage—if you will do it His way.

Living happily ever after might be the stuff of fairy tales. But happily *even* after? That can be your reality.

ESSENTIALS FOR HUSBANDS AND WIVES

Nevertheless let each one of you in particular so love his
own wife as himself, and let the wife *see* that she respects her
husband. (Ephesians 5:33)

Without fail, our smoke alarm goes off in the middle of the
night when the batteries are running low. It never seems
to go off at 4:00 in the afternoon. By the time I'm finished
dealing with the alarm in the middle of the night, I am not
feeling very positive about smoke alarms. But I also realize
that we need smoke alarms because they warn us of imminent
danger.

The problem is that many of us don't pay much attention to
alarms anymore because we hear them so often. When we hear a
car alarm go off in a parking lot, do we call the police? No. Often
it isn't going off because the car is being broken into; it's going
off because someone has forgotten where they parked.

I think there are some alarms going off in some marriages
today as well. But husbands and wives aren't paying any attention. But they need to, because there is a right and a wrong way
to have a successful marriage. If you don't work aggressively on
your marriage, if you aren't proactive about keeping it strong,

then it will default to a weakened state—and sometimes to a crisis state, depending on how far you let it go.

Marriage doesn't have a life all its own. Having a happy, strong, and lasting marriage is no accident. A strong marriage is that way because a husband and wife have applied effort.

The longer you do marriage God's way, the richer and the better your marriage becomes. I can say that from personal experience, from more than forty years of marriage, and also from knowing people who have been married for quite a long time. A happy, lasting marriage is doable.

Maybe you're newly married and think this doesn't apply to you. It *does* apply to you, because if you want a successful marriage down the road, it starts now. The evening of your life is determined by the morning of it. The end is determined by the beginning. If you want to be that sweet elderly couple walking through the park holding hands one day, then you must work on that now. You make the decision now—at this very moment—not later.

A strong and happy marriage is the result of obedience to God and His Word and laying aside this world's distorted take-it-or-leave-it concept of marriage.

One of the problems is we have allowed our culture and secular thinking to creep into the church. People who claim to be Christians are abandoning their marriages because they say they need to go "find" themselves. (Please don't ever say that.)

Jesus said that if you want a successful Christian life, you need to deny yourself and *lose yourself*—not go find yourself (see Matthew 16:24–25).

Marriage isn't about what the other person can do for you; it is about what you can do for the other person.

So often the problem in marriage is we are always reading each other's mail. Read your own mail. Do what God has told *you* to do. Husband, don't tell your wife what she is supposed to do. Wife, don't tell your husband where he is falling short. Focus on your own role in the marriage. If a husband and wife would each do their own part, what a difference it would make.

As a pastor who has counseled numerous couples over the years, I've discovered that everyone thinks their marital problems are unique. They really aren't. It's the same old issues popping up again and again. There are solutions for them if a man and woman will commit themselves to doing their marriage God's way. By God's power and obedience to the principles found in His Word, a couple can have a blessed, strong, and vibrant marriage.

But we have to go back to God's original design. In the last chapter, we looked at two operative words in a marriage: *leave* and *cleave.* These are two important things every couple needs to do. It means leaving all other relationships and making your marriage the most important part of your life, next to your relationship with God Himself. It also means holding on to each other.

Storms will come. And if you don't have a good foundation in your marriage, it will collapse. Having remodeled our kitchen due to flooding, I can tell you that it's more difficult to remodel a house while you're living in it than it is to start building from the ground up. It is a lot easier to build it right the first time.

If you are not married yet, get this right. If you are a newlywed, there is still time to lay this foundation the right way. If you are a little bit further down the road and are having problems, then you may need to go back and do some remodeling. Granted, it will be more of a challenge, but it beats the alternative, which is the destruction of your home.

If your marriage is strong and vibrant right now, I hope what you read will encourage and bolster you. If there is some big trouble underneath what looks like a wonderful exterior, I hope you will gain a biblical perspective to shore up that foundation.

Maybe your marriage is literally hanging by a thread. Maybe you're actually headed for divorce. I hope you will change your course and not abandon ship. There is hope for every hurting marriage. I like the acronym HOPE: Holding on with patient expectation. Hold on. Don't give up. You can do this with God's help.

FOUR WORDS FOR HUSBANDS

First, I have something to share with husbands. I want to give you husbands four words that will change your marriage. (And no, they are not *here's my credit card*.) We find them in Ephesians 5, where Paul writes, "Husbands, love your wives" (verse 25).

Four times in verses 25 to 33, husbands are told to love their wives. And how are we to love them? "Just as Christ also loved the church and gave Himself for her" (verse 25).

Yes, it is a tall order. But many—if not most—marriages are in trouble because men are unwilling to obey this simple and direct command from God: "Husbands, love your wives, just as Christ also loved the church and gave Himself for her."

The word Paul used here for *love* is the Greek word *agape.* It's a commonly used word in the New Testament, including in 1 John 4:8, which says that "God is love."

It's also the word used in John 3:16, where Jesus said, "For God so loved the world that he gave his one and only Son, that whoever believes in him shall not perish but have eternal life" (NIV). The same word is used in Galatians 5:22, which talks about the fruit of the Spirit: "But the Holy Spirit produces this kind of fruit in our lives: love, joy, peace, patience, kindness, goodness, faithfulness" (NLT). And this is something that God has placed in a believer's life already.

Maybe you're thinking, *I don't feel this love.*

You may not feel it, but it's there. The Bible tells us, "The love of God has been poured out in our hearts by the Holy Spirit who was given to us" (Romans 5:5).

One of the themes of Ephesians, as you may recall, is what God has done for us. God has given you this love.

I don't think we understand what love is in our culture anymore because we use the word to describe our feelings for everything. We love everything from sushi to our dogs to our husband or wife. And we mean different things in each instance. That is part of the problem.

The Greek language, however, has distinct words for love. First, there is *eros*, from which we get the word *erotic*. This refers to physical love, sexual attraction. *Eros* is expressed sexually and in the safety and boundaries of a Christian marriage, between a man and a woman. We are told very clearly in Scripture that you should only find this fulfillment from your spouse. Proverbs 5:15 says, "Drink water from your own well—share your love only with your wife" (NLT). Eros has its place.

But a problem with *eros* is that it's effectively a selfish love. This kind of love says, "I find you attractive. I want you. I want something from you."

That brings us to *phileo*, from which we get our English words *philanthropy* and *Philadelphia*. It is the idea of love shown through action. It is also a give-and-take kind of love that effectively says, "I will do something for you. You do something for me. We're friends." A man can have *phileo* love for a man, and a woman can have *phileo* love for a woman. It is brotherly and sisterly love.

Wives are specifically told in Titus 2 to *phileo* their husbands. This is a love that comes as a result of the pleasure or delight one draws from the object loved. You may like to be around certain people because they make you laugh or you find them interesting. They are great companions. That is *phileo*.

Then there is *agape*, which I've already mentioned. This is love on more of a spiritual plane. It's a sacrificial love that says, "I will love you no matter what you do."

Agape is different from the other loves, however. While *eros* says, "I want this from you," and *phileo* says, "I want this from you, but I will give something to you as well," *agape* says, "I don't want anything. I just love you."

Every one of these loves has its place in the marriage. But when Paul wrote, "Husbands, love your wives," he used the word *agape*.

In our culture, love is always object oriented. Our culture says, "I love you because you are lovable," or "I love you because you are attractive," or "I love you because you are smart."

People magazine publishes an annual issue of the world's most beautiful people, not the world's most unattractive people. We love lovable people

As time passes in your marriage, you get to know your spouse like no one else does. And you will discover that he or she can do unlovable things. That is just human nature. He or she will age, just as you will age. But it isn't an option to trade in your spouse on the newest model. You want a love that will last a lifetime.

In his excellent book on marriage, *Love Life for Every Married Couple*, Dr. Ed Wheat gives a fantastic definition of how *agape* love works:

> Even in the best of marriages unlovable traits show up in both partners. And in every marriage, sooner or later, a need arises that can be met only by unconditional love. *Agape* is the answer for all the woundings of marriage. . . . Agape is the Divine solution for marriages populated by imperfect human beings![1]

Marriages populated by imperfect human beings . . . that would be your marriage and mine.

God's Definition of Love

Our culture doesn't know what love is. Don't look to songs. Don't look to movies. Instead, look to the Bible for God's definition of love. We find a beautiful one in 1 Corinthians 13:

> Love is patient and kind. Love is not jealous or boastful or proud or rude. It does not demand its own way. It is not irritable, and it keeps no record of being wronged. It does not rejoice about injustice but rejoices whenever the truth wins out. Love never gives up, never loses faith, is always hopeful, and endures through every circumstance. (verses 4–7 NLT)

This is more a definition of what love *does* rather than what love *is*. Look at the above passage and put in your own name where the word *love* appears. Whose name best fits there? There is only one name that fits perfectly, and that is Jesus. Essentially, these verses are a portrait of Jesus Christ.

The love described in 1 Corinthians 13 isn't abstract or passive; it's active. It doesn't just *feel* patient; it *is* patient. Love doesn't just *feel* kind feelings; it *does* kind things.

Don't wait until you feel something. Just start doing it. The emotions will catch up. If a husband would take these verses alone and start applying them to his life, it would change his marriage.

Be Patient

Love is patient. If you really love your wife, you will be patient with her. When 1 Corinthians 13 says that "love is patient," it also could be translated, "Love is long-tempered." This word is common in the New Testament and is almost exclusively used in reference to being patient with people rather than being patient with circumstances or events.

It is not the idea of being patient when you are waiting at a traffic light or being patient with a line you are stuck in. This speaks of patience with people in particular. Yes, sometimes you will be taken advantage of. But you love again and again.

Show Kindness and Tenderness

Love is kind. Just as patience will take anything from others, kindness will give anything to others. The problem is that at first we show love in a relationship. When you first took your lady out on a date, you were kind to her, weren't you? You dressed up to the best of your ability. You told her she looked beautiful. You opened the door of the car for her to get in. Then, when you went to the restaurant, you held the door open for her. When you got to the table, you pulled out the chair.

Now that you have been married for a while, things have changed a little. You don't open the car door for her anymore. You do pull out the chair in the restaurant—you just don't put it back in. And when she falls on the floor, you laugh. Things have changed. You start taking her for granted.

Love is kind. This is the love that God wants us to have. It has been said that if you treat your wife like a thoroughbred, you never will end up with a nag.

Maybe you've been complaining that your wife isn't being the wife you want her to be. But are you being the husband that you ought to be?

Why do we, as the church, submit to Jesus Christ? Why do we do what He tells us to do? It's because His love won us over. As Romans 2:4 points out, "Don't you see how wonderfully kind, tolerant, and patient God is with you? Does this mean nothing to you? Can't you see that his kindness is intended to turn you from your sin?" (NLT). He showed us kindness. He showed us unconditional love. He never stopped loving us. Finally it melted our rebellious hearts, and we turned to Him. Now we follow Him because we trust Him.

Husband, if you would love your wife that way, you would be amazed at how she would respond. I believe that husbands hold the key to a flourishing marriage. I'm not excusing wives. But I am saying that husbands need to take the lead. Husbands need to be the initiators: "Love your wives, just as Christ also loved the church" (Ephesians 5:25).

By the way, this love shows itself practically, in little things, like surprising her with a gift. Find out what she likes. Pay attention. When you walk through a store with her, take note when she notices something. Then go back and get that for her later. Surprise her with it. Show your love in tangible ways.

Proverbs 31 says, "Her children arise and call her blessed; her husband also, and he praises her" (verse 28 NIV). When was the last time you praised your wife in front of your kids or even a stranger? Love her and celebrate her. Never denigrate her. Never make fun of your spouse in front of someone else.

Do the tangible, obvious things to show your love for your wife. And tell your wife that you love her. Even a hug and a kiss can go a long way.

In fact, research has shown that giving your wife a kiss might even help you live longer. A German group of psychologists, physicians, and insurance companies worked together on a research project to find the secret to long life and success. Do you know what they discovered? Men who kissed their wife each morning missed less work due to illness, and they earned 20 to 30 percent more income than nonkissers.

Love is kind. Show love to your wife in tangible ways.

Don't Boast

Love is not boastful or proud. If you love your wife, don't boast about it; just do it. Don't strut around and remind your wife of everything you do for her. She probably knows already. Don't boast about it.

Show Respect for Her

Love is not rude. If you love your wife, show respect for her. Some husbands have better manners toward complete strangers than they do toward the woman who is bone of their bones and flesh of their flesh. Some husbands will open a door for a stranger, yet they couldn't be bothered to help their wife unload the groceries when she gets home.

Don't Be Harsh

Love does not demand its own way. It is not irritable. If you love your wife, don't be harsh with her. *Agape* love is not easily provoked, which means it is not easily aroused to anger.

I was raised in a home where my mom got drunk every night. The routine would be having a few drinks at home. Next, it would be going out to dinner, coming home drunk, and drinking more. Then the screaming would begin. Then the throwing would begin. One time my mom almost died as a result of an argument she had with her husband at the time. In a drunken rage, he hit her on the head with a wooden figure, knocking her unconscious. I know what it's like to live in that environment. It's very traumatizing for a child.

Don't do that to your kids. If you have a disagreement with your spouse, and those times will come, don't do it in front of your kids. And don't ever ask your kids to take sides in an argument. Use a little self-control. If you can't calm down, just walk away. You need to come back later when you can be calm about it.

Love is not harsh. The Bible says, "Do not let the sun go down while you are still angry" (Ephesians 4:26 NIV). I heard about a couple who decided to put that verse into practice and never go to bed angry with each other. After years of marriage, someone asked how that worked out.

The husband said, "Pretty good. But sometimes it was a little rough sitting up all night."

Don't go to bed mad at each other. Don't be harsh with your wife.

Believe the Best

Love keeps no record of being wronged. If you love your wife, you always will believe the best, not the worst, about her. The New King James Version says that love "thinks no evil" (1 Corinthians 13:5). In Greek, this is a bookkeeping phrase that means "to calculate or enter into a ledger, a permanent record that can be consulted when needed."

Maybe you're having an argument with your wife, and you say, "I remember when you said this. . . ."

"When was that?"

"Twenty years ago."

You shouldn't be keeping a record of those things. Learn to forgive. Ruth Graham once said the secret of a successful marriage is "two good forgivers." Learn how to forgive and put things behind you.

Endure the Tough Times

Love endures through every circumstance. If you really love your wife, you will make it through the rough patches. *Agape* love endures all things. It refuses to surrender. It will not stop believing or hoping. Love simply will not stop loving.

When some friction arises in a marriage, some people are so quick to opt out. Don't do that. There are extenuating circumstances where separation might be necessary, such as any kind of violence, any kind of hitting, or some activity going on in the home that is detrimental to the spouse or the children. But I would highly recommend that a husband or wife does this with pastoral counseling and guidance.

On the other hand, it is not grounds for separation if you're simply tired of or irritated by your spouse. That excuse is used far too often.

I like how *The Message* puts it: "Love . . . trusts God always, always looks for the best, never looks back, but keeps going to the end" (1 Corinthians 13:4, 7).

EMPOWERED BY THE HOLY SPIRIT

You might read this as a husband and think, *Who can live like this? Who can love like this?*

Well, *you* can, because the love of God has been placed in your heart by the Holy Spirit. God will give you the power to do what He has called you to do.

It's time to step up and be the man of God the Lord has called you to be. It's time to love your wife as Christ loved the church.

How did Jesus love the church? He came to this earth and died on a cross for us. The Bible says that "while we were still sinners, Christ died for us" (Romans 5:8). He shed His blood for us when we were living in rebellion against Him.

His love for us is so beautifully shown as He hung on the cross and said, "Father, forgive them, for they do not know what they do" (Luke 23:34).

Effectively, He was saying, "Father, they have committed a sin that is so dark and so evil, they don't even comprehend how wicked it is. Lord, forgive them. They did nothing to merit that."

Yes, that is God's love. God loved each one of us so much that He sent Jesus to die on the cross. And Jesus laid His life down for us. *Husbands, love your wives, just as Christ also loved the church.*

If I were to sum up in one word the greatest problem in marriages today it would be this—*Selfishness.* We make it all about ourselves and never about the other. If I were to sum up in one word the solution to failing marriages today it would be *Selflessness.*

GOD'S WORD TO WIVES

If you're a married woman reading this today, I want to talk to you about how to get a new husband. Don't misunderstand. I am not suggesting that you trade in your existing husband on a new one. But I do want to talk to you about things you can do so he will become a new man.

But before you can turn your husband into a new man, you need to think about becoming a new woman. Some women work so hard to make good husbands, they never manage to make good wives.

Let's see what the Bible says about how to get a new husband:

> In the same way, you wives must accept the authority of your husbands. Then, even if some refuse to obey the Good News, your godly lives will speak to them without any words. They will be won over by observing your pure and reverent lives.
>
> Don't be concerned about the outward beauty of fancy hairstyles, expensive jewelry, or beautiful

clothes. You should clothe yourselves instead with the beauty that comes from within, the unfading beauty of a gentle and quiet spirit, which is so precious to God. (1 Peter 3:1–4 NLT)

Contextually, this passage is talking about reaching a nonbelieving husband. Maybe you find yourself in that situation right now. Maybe you married him even though he wasn't a Christian. Or, maybe you both were non-Christians when you got married, and then you became a Christian. Whatever the case, you might be wondering if you should stay with this guy because he is hard to deal with. Maybe he even has made it hard for you to be a Christian and has harassed you for your faith.

Maybe you've met someone at church and think you've heard the Lord say, "Dump your heathen husband and marry the cute Christian guy."

Trust me, the Lord didn't say that to you. If you want to know what God says to a Christian woman who is married to a non-Christian man, then you have His Word in 1 Peter 3.

Or, perhaps you are a godly woman married to a nominally godly man. Technically he believes in Jesus Christ. He has put his faith in Christ. But he is not a spiritual leader, and you are wondering how to get him to lead more effectively. In 1 Peter 3, you'll find principles for doing that.

Be the Best Version of Yourself

If you want to get a new husband, then you want to be the best version of yourself that you can be.

First, you want to be a *godly* woman. The Bible speaks of the woman of virtue in Proverbs 31. We usually think of *virtue* or *virtuous* as a feminine word. But in the Bible, it is also used to describe men. It is a word that speaks of purity, strength, force, and value. So you want to be a woman like that. You want to be a balanced woman. You want to be a pure woman. You want to be a strong woman. This is a woman who is balanced. This is a woman who is beautiful on the inside as well as the outside.

Have you ever looked at the covers of women's magazines? It seems like the emphasis is always on how to lose weight, new hairstyles, sex, or horoscopes. It is all on the outward. Can you imagine if the cover of one of these women's magazines featured the headline "How to Be a Godly Woman" or "Working on Your Spiritual Life" or "How to Get More Out of Your Devotions"?

We never will see that because there is no emphasis on the inner person. It is all about the outward appearance. The emphasis is on all the wrong things.

That is not the way that a godly woman, a virtuous woman, should live. Those who consume themselves with outward appearance alone will waste their lives. The truth is that time will pass and gravity eventually will kick in. It is just reality. In time, that striking beauty will fade. Then what will be left? If that is all you live for, what will be left is an empty, shallow woman who has thrown her life way.

Here is the great thing about being a godly woman. Maybe you're not as beautiful as you once were, but in other ways, you are more beautiful because you have an inner beauty.

There is something very interesting about inner beauty that makes the outer beauty even more appealing. There is that light, that virtue, that purity coming from the inside. The Bible says in Proverbs 31:30, "Charm is deceptive, and beauty does not last; but a woman who fears the Lord will be greatly praised" (NLT).

The godly woman focuses primarily on the internal, but she also doesn't neglect the external. Don't go too far either way.

In 1 Peter 3:3, women are told, "Do not let your adornment be merely outward." The word *adornment* comes from the Greek word *cosmos*. This is the same word from which we get our English word *cosmetic*. This verse is a warning for the woman who majors on externals while ignoring the internal. Peter then mentions "putting on fine apparel." This could be better translated "the frequent changing of clothing." The idea is that of a woman who is constantly changing her clothes to impress other people.

In the first century, the women of Rome were excessive in this regard. When it came to the outward appearance, they really went for it. They wore their hair piled high in elaborate hairstyles. They wore rings on their fingers and toes. The wealthy women lived pampered lives. Peter was responding to that culture.

However, the Bible isn't saying that a woman shouldn't be attractive. That is why my first point is to be the best version of yourself that you can be. There is a place for that. The woman described in Proverbs 31 owned expensive clothing (see verse 22). There is nothing wrong with having beautiful clothes. There is nothing wrong with being a beautiful woman on the outside.

Esther, who ended up saving the Jewish people, won a beauty contest. Clearly she had outward beauty as well as inner beauty.

Don't be preoccupied with the outside, but don't neglect it, either. In 1 Timothy 4:8, Paul wrote, "For bodily exercise profits a little, but godliness is profitable for all things, having promise of the life that now is and of that which is to come."

This doesn't mean we shouldn't do anything physically. This doesn't mean we should sit around and become obese. Notice that Paul said, "Bodily exercise profits *a little*" (emphasis added). There is a place for exercise. There is a place for a proper diet. But don't make these things what you're all about.

Sometimes in the name of spirituality, Christian women neglect their appearance. They think, *I'm married now, so why should I bother?*

That is not a good mind-set to have. Be the best version of yourself that you can be.

Be Respectful

If you want to get a new husband, respect him. In Ephesians 5:33 we read, "Nevertheless let each one of you in particular so love his own wife as himself, and let the wife see that she respects her husband."

Interestingly, husbands are told to *love* their wives, and wives are told to *respect* their husbands. This is not to say that a husband shouldn't respect his wife. Nor is it to say that a wife shouldn't love her husband. But the Bible specifically says a husband is to love his wife, and a wife is to respect her husband.

Just as a husband is to love his wife, even if she does not respect and submit to him, so a wife should respect her husband, even if he does not love her as she wants him to. Dr. Emerson Eggerichs writes in his excellent book *Love and Respect*, "When a husband feels disrespected, it is especially hard to love his wife. When a wife feels unloved, it is especially hard to respect her husband. . . . When a husband feels disrespected, he has a natural tendency to react in ways that seem unloving to his wife. . . . When a wife feels unloved, she has a natural tendency to react in ways that feel disrespectful to her husband."[2]

What is the solution? Again, stop reading each other's mail. Stop telling your husband what he is supposed to do. Just focus on what you are supposed to do.

God is not calling on the wife to *feel* respect; He is commanding her to show respectful behavior.

"Well, I'm not feeling that," a wife might say.

Do it anyway. I think, in time, your emotions will catch up with your actions because you're doing the right thing. Don't make this all about emotions. Just do what God tells you to do. It might feel unnatural or counterintuitive, but just do it.

Remember when you were first learning to drive? You had to think about everything: *change lanes . . . look over your shoulder . . . brake.* But after you drove for a while, it got easier. Before long, you didn't even have to think about it. You just got in the car and drove.

In the same way, simply start showing respect to your husband. Just start doing the right thing. Before long, you may not even have to think about it.

It reminds me of a story I read about a woman who wanted to divorce her husband and went to see an attorney. She said, "I hate my husband, and I really want to hurt him. Give me some advice."

The attorney thought about it for a few moments and said, "This will make him so miserable. Here's what I want you to do. For the next three months, don't criticize him. Speak only well of him and to him. Build him up. Every time he does something nice, commend him for it. Most of all, tell him how much you respect and appreciate him. Don't forget to smother him with affection as well. Do this for three months. Then, when he is least expecting it, nail him and tell him you're divorcing him. He won't see it coming."

So for the next three months, the woman showed her husband respect, affection, and love, and she commended him for every right thing he did.

After the three months were up, the attorney called the woman and said, "All right. When are we going to get those papers filed?"

"What papers?" the woman said. "We're going on our second honeymoon."

She simply started doing the right thing, and it changed her marriage.

Submit to His Leadership

If you want to get a new husband, submit to his leadership. Many women bristle at the thought of this. I believe that's primarily because they don't understand it. This is not about superiority or inferiority. It is about sacrifice. It is about putting the needs of your mate before your own. Ephesians 5:21 says, "Submitting *to one another* in the fear of God" (emphasis added). The Greek word translated *submitting* is a military term that speaks of getting underneath someone and holding him up.

Going back to 1 Peter 3:1, "In the same way, you wives must accept the authority of your husbands. Then, even if some refuse to obey the Good News, your godly lives will speak to them without any words" (NLT). Paul teaches the same thing in Ephesians 5:22: "Wives, submit to your own husbands, as to the Lord." Yet this is something a lot of women choke on.

A wife should be her husband's number one fan. A husband should be his wife's number one fan. You help each other up and hold each other up. You put his needs above your own. Submit to one another in the fear of God.

Let Your Conduct Do the Talking

If you want to get a new husband, win him over by your actions, not by your words. Notice 1 Peter 3 says, "Even if some [husbands] refuse to obey the Good News, your godly lives will speak to them without any words. They will be won over by observing your pure and reverent lives" (verses 1–2 NLT). I believe women communicate more effectively and intuitively than men. I say this as an observation, not a criticism. You can watch five women having a conversation in which everyone is talking at the same time, and somehow they understand each other. This mystifies men.

A conversation between men usually goes something like this.

"Hey, how's it going?"

"It's going pretty well. How about you?"

"Pretty good."

That is typical of a guy talking to a guy.

Dr. James Dobson has said that men are born with the same amount of brain cells as women, but at an early age, a male's brain is flooded with testosterone, which destroys a lot of brain cells. Thus, men typically are not able to communicate as well as women do.[3]

And often when a woman says one thing, a man hears another. For example, when a wife says to her husband, "Let's stop and ask for directions," her husband hears, "You are not a man."

When a wife asks for the remote, her husband hears, "Let's watch something that will bore me beyond belief."

When a wife says, "I need some money to redecorate," he hears, "Let's flush a lot of money down the toilet."

When she says, "Are you listening to me?" he hears, "Blah, blah, blah, blah, blah."

Here's the challenge for women. If your husband isn't a Christian, or if he isn't the believer he should be, try to reach him more by the way you live than by what you say.

I think a woman is a persuader by nature. This can be positive or negative, depending on how she uses it. We all know what happened in the Garden of Eden. I am not blaming Eve (even though Adam did). She played a role in Adam's sin, but Adam was complicit and chose to disobey God.

If a wife would take her ability to persuade and use it in a godly way, the Lord could use her in a powerful and effective way in the life of her husband.

Nagging drives a husband crazy. Solomon, who had three hundred wives and seven hundred concubines, had a lot to say about nagging. He wrote, "A nagging spouse is a leaky faucet" (Proverbs 19:13 msg). Have you ever been awakened by the sound of continuous dripping? You can't go back to sleep until you get up, find it, and stop it. That is what nagging is like to a husband.

Solomon also said, "Better to live in a desert than with a quarrelsome and nagging wife" (Proverbs 21:19 NIV). A wife who always quarrels and scolds her husband can really get him upset. In fact, it's been said that a wife who henpecks her husband is likely to find him listening to some other chick. I know that husbands mess up. I know they don't do all the things their wives want them to. But does your husband do *anything* right? Is he working hard? Is he providing for you? Is he protecting you? How about balancing your critiques with some compliments as well? Sometimes wives emphasize only the negative about their husbands and never the positive. Yet what does Ephesians 5:33 say? "Let the wife see that she respects her husband."

Husbands and wives have unique roles in a marriage. Just focus on what God has called you do to. If you, as a wife, would apply these principles and do your part in helping your husband be the best man he can be, I think you would be amazed to find that you have a new husband.

A REFLECTION OF CHRIST AND HIS CHURCH

God has taken the Christian marriage and has effectively said to a lost world, "This is a reflection of My love for My church. Do you want to know how much I love My church? Notice the way that a Christian man loves his wife. That is how much I love My church. Do you want to know how much My church loves Me? Watch that Christian woman and the way she loves her husband. That is how My church loves Me."

How are you doing on that? As followers of Christ, we are a reflection of Him.

That is why it's incredibly tragic when a Christian marriage unravels. Are we no different than our secular culture? Do we not have the Spirit of God living inside us? Do we not have the Word of God telling us what to do?

Then why can't we make an extra effort, go the extra mile, and see what the Lord will do?

We can—and we must—do this.

PART 3

FIGHT

14

THIS MEANS WAR

This is no afternoon athletic contest that we'll walk away
from and forget about in a couple of hours. This is for keeps,
a life-or-death fight to the finish against the Devil and all his
angels.(Ephesians 6:12 msg)

Only two decades had passed since World War I when another global conflict began taking form. Germany was conquering territory, and there were conflicts in Asia as well. The United States was helping its friend and ally, Great Britain, but wasn't officially engaged in the conflict. That is, until December 7, 1941, when the Japanese bombed Pearl Harbor and murdered 2,403 Americans. The next day, the United States declared war on Japan and officially entered World War II. Afterward, Japanese Admiral Isoroku Yamamoto said, "I fear all we have done is to awaken a sleeping giant and fill him with a terrible resolve."[1]

If you are a Christian, war has been declared on you—by Satan. Are you going to fight back? Or, will you climb into a little foxhole somewhere and hope he doesn't hurt you?

I have some bad news for you: The devil wants to destroy you. It's time to step up. It's time to do more than merely defend yourself. It's time to do more than hold your ground. It's time

221

to take new ground and move forward. This is called spiritual warfare.

The day you put your faith in Jesus Christ, the battle began. It has been said that conversion has made our hearts a battlefield. Believers may be known by their inward warfare as well as their inward peace. Anyone who chooses to be on the side of the Lord Jesus Christ will face severe opposition from Satan and his followers. And those who refuse to fight surely will fall in the heat of battle.

What would the world look like today if the United States hadn't responded to Japan's attack on Pearl Harbor? What would the world look like today if the United States had allowed Germany to continue its march across Europe and its slaughter of Jewish people? It would be a much different world today—and a much worse one.

In the same way, what would our lives as Christians look like if we don't do anything in response to Satan's attacks? They would look like defeat.

It is time to arm ourselves and get ready for the battle.

THE CHRISTIAN LIFE IS A BATTLEGROUND

The Bible often uses conflict in battle to describe the Christian life. Paul exhorted Timothy to "endure hardship as a good soldier of Jesus Christ" (2 Timothy 2:3).

Paul also said in 2 Timothy 4:7, "I have fought the good fight, I have finished the race, I have kept the faith," reminding us that the Christian life is not a playground; it's a battleground.

And he encouraged Timothy to "fight the good fight of the faith. Take hold of the eternal life to which you were called when you made your good confession in the presence of many witnesses" (1 Timothy 6:12 NIV).

The good news is that although we are in this battle, we ultimately win in the end. (I have read the last page of the Bible.) We may lose a battle here and there, or a skirmish occasionally, but we will win the ultimate war. We have God's word on that.

Jesus said the gates of hell would not prevail against the church (see Matthew 16:18). An ancient military tactic commonly used by armies was to break down the gates of the enemy's fortress with a battering ram. The point of entry was the gate, and therefore, attackers had to batten down the gate.

When Jesus said the gates of hell would not prevail against the church, He was saying that as we march forward as His followers, we will break down that gate, and we will win. Ultimately, we will not be overcome.

When I was a brand-new Christian, other believers at my high school told me, "Greg, be careful. You will be tempted by the Devil."

It caught me by surprise. No one said anything about a devil when I became a Christian. I said, "How will I know when I am being tempted?"

"You'll know."

And they were right.

I went to my next class, where there happened to be a very attractive girl. I had noticed her before, but she had never noticed me. I didn't think she even knew I existed. But after class that day, she walked over to me and said, "Hi. What's your name?"

I temporarily forgot my name.

She said, "You know, you are really cute."

I thought, *What? Are you talking to me?*

"My parents are away for the weekend," she continued. "I have a cabin in the mountains. Would you like to come and spend the weekend with me?"

I thought, *This never happens to me.* And then it hit me. This is what my new Christian friends had warned me about. This was temptation.

I said no to that girl, even though I walked away wondering what I had just done. But I was glad I turned her down. That day, I learned that temptation comes in attractive packages.

The Bible says, "Blessed is the man who endures temptation; for when he has been approved, he will receive the crown of life which the Lord has promised to those who love Him" (James 1:12). It's hard to resist temptation in the moment. But afterward you'll be glad you turned that temptation down.

It isn't a sin to be tempted. It is only a sin when you give in to the temptation. And maybe you're being tempted because you're doing something right.

Remember all the calamity that came upon God's servant Job? It wasn't because he was doing something wrong. It was because he was doing something right. God was bragging on him in Heaven, saying to Satan and the other angels, "Have you noticed my servant Job? He is the finest man in all the earth. He is blameless—a man of complete integrity. He fears God and stays away from evil" (Job 1:8 NLT). The Devil went after Job, and God allowed it to a certain degree. It is because Job was walking with God that he came under attack. The same is true of us.

I think the Devil looks at some people and says, "Why should I mess with them? I already have them where I want them. But this Christian over here is really irritating me. That person is praying all of the time. This person is sharing her faith all the time. This other Christian is making a difference in his little world. I've got to stop them. I'm going to turn up the heat of temptation in their lives."

We don't have to constantly be victims. So often we are subject to our moods and fluctuating emotions. We are easily defeated on the spiritual battlefield. But it doesn't have to be that way.

ARM YOURSELF

I want to share some biblical principles with you that literally can transform your Christian life. To be forewarned is to be forearmed. Please pay careful attention to what you read because the Devil doesn't want you to know these things. He doesn't want you to discover these truths that we are about to examine together.

So far, we have talked about living and loving as part of the Christian life. Now let's talk about fighting—fighting to win.

> Finally, my brethren, be strong in the Lord and in the power of His might. Put on the whole armor of God, that you may be able to stand against the wiles of the devil. For we do not wrestle against flesh and blood, but against principalities, against powers, against the rulers of the darkness of this age, against spiritual hosts of wickedness in the heavenly places. Therefore take up the whole armor of God, that you may be able to withstand

in the evil day, and having done all, to stand.
(Ephesians 6:10–13)

The words *put on* in verse 11 carry the idea of putting something on once and for all. It's a permanent kind of thing. It isn't
putting your armor on and then taking it off. Rather, you put it
on, and you keep it on.

The idea is that you must always have your guard up as a
Christian. This spiritual battle never ends. Wouldn't it be nice
if it did end occasionally? Wouldn't it be fantastic if we could
just have a break on Sundays—or better yet, if the Devil took an
entire month off?

I'm sorry, but he doesn't take a month off. He doesn't take a
week off. He doesn't take a day off. He doesn't even take an hour
off. (And, by the way, even if he did, we would still get ourselves
into trouble.) The spiritual battle ends when we get to Heaven,
not before then.

We have to keep our guard up because the Devil is always
looking for an opportunity. The Bible says, "Therefore let him
who thinks he stands take heed lest he fall" (1 Corinthians 10:12).

The very moment you lower your guard is when you are
going to get hit. The Devil knows that, and he is looking for those
opportunities. That is why we always have to be armed and aware.

YES, THERE IS A DEVIL

Someone might say, "Oh please. The Devil? Really? Do you
actually believe there is a Devil?"

Yes, I do. In fact, the Devil is the obvious, and even logical,
explanation of the evil that runs rampant in our culture and world

today. People want to attribute the horrible things that are happening to many different roots. But they miss the most significant thing of all: There is a Devil. There is evil. And sometimes people simply do wicked and depraved things because Satan has gained control of them.

Psychologists will opine in interviews with the media, and others will offer their ideas about what the cause of these horrible thing may be. But the cause is evil. Evil is alive in the world, and it can penetrate any culture. It can penetrate any life. People may laugh off Satan, but he should be taken seriously.

It seems that we fall into two extremes when it comes to the Devil. C. S. Lewis summed it up perfectly when he said, "There are two equal and opposite errors into which our race can fall about the devils. One is to disbelieve in their existence. The other is to believe, and to feel an excessive and unhealthy interest in them. They themselves are equally pleased by both errors and hail a materialist or a magician with the same delight."[2]

We must never underestimate the Devil. He is a sly and skillful foe, and he has had years to perfect his craft.

A question that is often asked is why would a God of love create someone like the Devil? Technically, God did not create the Devil as we know Him. We are told in Genesis 1:31 that when God created the world, "Then God saw everything that He had made, and indeed it was very good. So the evening and the morning were the sixth day." This means that in the angelic world, there were no evil angels or demons yet.

But by the time we get to Genesis 3, we are introduced to Satan, who comes slithering up to Eve and tempts her at the Tree of the Knowledge of Good and Evil. But Satan wasn't always Satan. He once was a high-ranking angel known as Lucifer.

Sometime between the events of Genesis 1 and Genesis 3, there must have been a rebellion in the angelic world. We know from other passages that one-third of the angels of God went rogue. They rebelled against God and followed the leading of a powerful angel known as Lucifer.

The good news is that two-thirds of the angels are still on our side. That is a great thing to know. There are a lot of angels, and they are involved in our lives. The Scripture says they are "ministering spirits sent forth to minister to those who will inherit salvation" (Hebrews 1:14).

The Bible tells us that Lucifer was amazingly beautiful. He seemed to be in a position of great power and influence. In fact, Ezekiel 28 provides a graphic description of Lucifer before he fell:

> "You were the seal of perfection,
>
> full of wisdom and perfect in beauty.
>
> You were in Eden,
>
> the garden of God; . . .
>
> You were anointed as a guardian cherub,
>
> for so I ordained you.
>
> You were on the holy mount of God;
>
> you walked among the fiery stones.
>
> You were blameless in your ways
>
> from the day you were created
>
> till wickedness was found in you. . . ."
>
> (verses 12–15 NIV)

There are different kinds of angels: the cherubim, the seraphim, and archangels like Michael and Gabriel.

The cherubim are depicted in the Scriptures as powerful, majestic, angelic creatures who surround God's throne. In Genesis 3:24, we read that "after [God] drove the man out, he placed on the east side of the Garden of Eden cherubim and a flaming sword flashing back and forth to guard the way to the tree of life" (NIV).

Ezekiel 28:14 describes Lucifer as a "guardian cherub," so he appeared to be one of the cherubim at some point. But then he fell.

Why?

He was on the ultimate ego trip, if you will. He was referred to as "the seal of perfection." But his heart became proud because of his incredible beauty. He allowed his perfection to be the cause of his corruption.

Technically, Adam and Eve didn't commit the first sin. The first sin actually was committed by Lucifer when he became so enthralled with himself that he rebelled against God.

We find more details in Isaiah 14, where God says,

"How you are fallen from heaven,

O Lucifer, son of the morning!

How you are cut down to the ground,

You who weakened the nations!

For you have said in your heart:

'I will ascend into heaven,

I will exalt my throne above the stars of God;

I will also sit on the mount of the congregation

On the farthest sides of the north;

I will ascend above the heights of the clouds,

I will be like the Most High.'

Yet you shall be brought down to Sheol,

To the lowest depths of the Pit."

(verses 12–15)

Lucifer wasn't satisfied with worshiping God; he wanted to be worshiped himself. Once a beautiful, powerful angel, he rebelled against the Lord. Lucifer became Satan when he fell to Earth. And ever since, his goal has been to attack that which God loves.

Earlier I mentioned Job, who suffered a great deal of calamity in his life. God allowed this to occur, but it was the Devil who actually prompted them. We read in the book of Job about servants being murdered, goods being stolen, winds blowing, lightning striking, and houses falling. Interestingly, insurance agents would call some of those things "acts of God." But these actually were acts of Satan.

There was a hedge of protection around Job, which the Devil even acknowledged, yet the Devil was allowed a certain entry into Job's life. This shows us that although he is in a fallen state, Satan still has access into God's presence. The Bible describes him as "the accuser of our brethren, who accused them before our God day and night" (Revelation 12:10).

THE DEVIL'S LIMITS

Satan can do nothing in the life of the Christian unless God gives him permission.

Matthew's gospel gives an account of Jesus being met by two demon-possessed men, who cried out, "What have we to do with You, Jesus, You Son of God? Have You come here to torment us before the time?" (8:29). The demons asked permission to be sent into a nearby herd of swine. The pigs reacted by running over the side of a cliff. (That was the first case in history of deviled ham.) The point is, the demons had to first ask Jesus' permission.

We also find an occasion in the Gospels when Satan set his sights on Simon Peter. Jesus was hanging around with His disciples when He turned to Peter and said, "Simon, Simon! Indeed, Satan has asked for you, that he may sift you as wheat" (Luke 22:31).

Imagine how you would feel if Jesus were to say that to you.

But then Jesus continued, "But I have prayed for you, that your faith should not fail; and when you have returned to Me, strengthen your brethren" (verse 32). In other words, "Don't sweat it, buddy. I've got you covered."

This shows what a threat Peter was to Satan. But Satan simply couldn't go and take Peter out. He needed God's permission.

The next time Satan comes knocking at your door, I think the best thing to do is say, "Lord, would you mind getting that?" We don't want to face him in our strength. We're weak. We're vulnerable. Let Christ face him.

But we might wonder why God would even give Satan permission to bring trials and temptations into our lives.

There are many reasons God allows this. One is to make us more like Christ. Another is to show us our weakness and our need to depend on Him.

God never will give us more than we can handle. He always grades temptation to the fiber of our lives. He won't give us more than we can take. He knows what we're capable of facing. We don't, but He does.

The Devil has clear limitations. He is not God's equal. Some people might see God and the Devil as the yin and yang, the positive and the negative, like Darth Vader and Luke Skywalker with the Force. It isn't like that. Forget yin and yang. Forget the Force. God is all-powerful with no equal in the universe. Having said that, Satan has considerable power, but he has nothing near the power of God.

God is omnipotent, which means He is all-powerful. God is omniscient, which means He knows everything. God is omnipresent, which means He can be present everywhere at the same time.

Satan doesn't have any of these divine attributes. He is not omnipotent. He does have great power, more than any man and most angels. Yet he is nowhere the equal of God. Satan isn't omniscient. He has a powerful intellect, and from experience, he knows many things. He knows more than any human. But only God is all-knowing. Satan isn't omnipresent. He is an individual personality and can only be in one place at one time.

When we say things like, "The Devil is hassling me," or "Satan is really tempting me," that probably isn't technically true. It is doubtful that most of us would register on his radar to the extent he would come after us personally. That doesn't mean we don't get tempted or hassled. What it means is that he takes one of his demon powers, one of his minions, and he sends them to tempt you. They are doing his bidding. They have considerable power. But it is doubtful that the big guy himself would come after you. In effect, it was the same thing. But the Devil can be in only one place at one time.

THE DEVIL'S METHODS

The reason we need to put on the armor of God, Paul says, is so we "may be able to stand against the wiles of the devil" (Ephesians 6:11). I would encourage you to underline that in your Bible. The word *wiles* comes from the English word *method*. It carries the meaning of craftiness, cunning, and deception. The term is used in reference to a wild animal who cunningly stalks and then unexpectedly pounces on its prey. It is like an animal that pretends like it doesn't care, but is getting closer and closer. Then, it pounces on its prey.

That is what the Devil does. He sizes us up. He has his wiles. He has his strategies that he uses against us.

When Paul wrote in verse 12, "For we do not wrestle against flesh and blood, but against principalities, against powers, against the rulers of the darkness of this age, against spiritual hosts of wickedness in the heavenly places," the word translated *wrestle* is a Greek term that describes mortal hand-to-hand combat. It's a fight to the death. That is what we are engaged in with Satan. He wants to stop us from coming to Christ. Then, if we believe in Jesus, he wants to immobilize us somehow.

As I've mentioned already, he has a well-developed network of demons to do his dirty work. He took one-third of them with him. We know there are millions and millions of angels—more than Satan has—but he still has a considerable amount. There are many references in the Scriptures that refer to the Devil and his demons. In Matthew 12:24, Jesus refers to Satan as "Beelzebub" and "the ruler of the demons." The word *Beelzebub* means "lord of the flies," by the way. Then in Matthew 25:41, Jesus refers to "the devil and his angels." And Revelation 12:7 refers to "the dragon and his angels." These angels are fallen angels, or demons.

The purpose of demons seems to be twofold. They seek to hinder the purposes of God and to extend the kingdom and power of Satan. In fact, Paul wrote in 1 Thessalonians 2:18 that he wanted to go to a certain place, but Satan prevented him. He also wrote about a time when he died, went to Heaven, and saw amazing things. After this revelation, a messenger of Satan was sent to humble him. Paul said he pleaded with the Lord three times to take it away, but the Lord said, "My grace is sufficient for you, for my power is made perfect in weakness" (2 Corinthians 12:9 NIV). Paul said, "Therefore I will boast all the more gladly about my weaknesses, so that Christ's power may rest on me" (verse 10 NIV).

When God blesses a person in a powerful and significant way, when God elevates a person to great influence, you can be sure of one thing: he or she is under spiritual attack.

We need to pray for our spiritual leaders. It is very easy to criticize and judge them. It is very easy to attack them, or sometimes to envy them. But you don't know the price they personally pay. You don't know what they have to face. The Enemy attacks them in many ways. Sometimes God will allow things to keep that person humble and dependent upon God. That is what happened to Paul.

Any time you share the gospel, the Devil will be there to try to oppose it. In the parable of the sower, Jesus talked about the seed that was sown on the roadside, which the birds came and ate (see Matthew 13:4).

You know how that is. You go to an outdoor restaurant and realize the birds have figured out it's the place for free lunch. They hang around, and the moment you drop a fry, they swoop it right up. They might even come and take the fry right off your plate.

That is the picture Jesus gave in His parable. He said, "When anyone hears the word of the kingdom, and does not understand it, then the wicked one comes and snatches away what was sown in his heart" (Matthew 13:19).

The Devil will try to stop you from believing in Jesus. But if you do believe, then he will try to get you to compromise and immobilize you so you won't be a threat to him.

Although he can hassle you, although he can tempt you, he cannot control you. No Christian should ever say, "The Devil made me do it." The Devil can't make you do anything that you don't want to do. If you fall into some sin, don't say the Devil made you do it. Say the Devil tempted you, and you went for it. You had a part in that.

While the Christian is surrounded by a wall of protection given by God, a non-Christian has no wall of protection at all. A non-Christian essentially is a sitting duck. For example, when a non-Christian gets into occultism or mysticism, he or she can open the door to the Devil.

Even drugs can open that door. Our English word *pharmacy* is derived from the Greek word *pharmakeia*. *Pharmakeia* basically speaks of the use of hallucinogens. In ancient times, people would use these to worship their pagan deities. The Bible warns against using these drugs and getting into that lifestyle.

The only power that can stop Satan is Jesus Christ. Nothing else. A crucifix will not stop him. Holy water will not stop him. A silver bullet will not stop him. A string of garlic around your neck won't keep him and his demons away, but I'm pretty sure it will keep your friends away. The only power the Devil respects is the power of Jesus Christ.

In addition to demons who do his dirty work, Satan has two close allies: the world and the flesh. Thus, the primary enemies a Christian faces every day are the world, the flesh, and the Devil.

The world is the culture we live in. It isn't the Earth in and of itself, but our culture and its beliefs, the mentality of people today. John wrote, "We know that we are of God, and the whole world lies under the sway of the wicked one" (1 John 5:19).

The flesh is the sinful nature. It isn't so much your physical body, per se, but your sinful inclinations, your appetites. These are the foes we have to deal with every day. John summed it up this way: "For all that is in the world—the lust of the flesh, the lust of the eyes, and the pride of life—is not of the Father but is of the world" (1 John 2:16). Every temptation you've ever experienced would fit into one of these categories: the lust of the flesh, the lust of the eyes, and the pride of life.

In the Garden of Eden, Satan said to Eve, "You will not surely die. For God knows that in the day you eat of it your eyes will be opened, and you will be like God, knowing good and evil" (Genesis 3:4–5).

In other words, "Eve, you will be like a goddess. Go for it."

The Bible says, "So when the woman saw that the tree was good for food, that it was pleasant to the eyes, and a tree desirable to make one wise, she took of its fruit and ate. She also gave to her husband with her, and he ate" (verse 6).

The fruit looked good. It tasted good. It seemed good at the time. That is how temptation comes. There is the lust of the eyes: Eve *saw* the tree was good for food. Then there is the lust of the flesh: Eve saw the tree was good for *food*. Finally, there is the pride of life: Eve saw the tree was desirable *to make one wise*. We fall to one or more of these things when we get into temptation.

Thankfully, God hasn't left us in the dark when it comes to overcoming the Devil and his demons.

A WINNING STRATEGY

Recognize It's a Spiritual Battle

First, let's recognize we are in a spiritual battle, and it has to be fought with spiritual weapons. You fight fire with fire.

Realize We Can't Do It on Our Own

Next, let's realize that Satan is a superbeing who is far more than we can ever handle. We cannot face him in our own strength. We want to stay as far from him as possible and as close to God as we can. Ephesians 4:27 says, "Do not give the devil a foothold" (NIV). We want to keep our distance.

In Acts, chapter 19, we find a story about a group of guys in Ephesus who are described as exorcists and identified as the "seven sons of Sceva." They saw the power of God demonstrated through Paul and thought it was some kind of a magic formula they could use. This little group tried to cast out a demon by "the Jesus whom Paul preaches" (verse 13).

The demon replied, "Jesus I know, and Paul I know; but who are you?" (verse 15). The man with the demon leaped on them, overpowered them, and attacked them with such violence that they fled from the house, "naked and wounded" (verse 16).

That is what happens when you try to deal with demons in your own strength. You'll get beat up. You don't have any way to overcome them. But if we come in the power of God, it's an entirely different story.

Resolve to Stand in God's Strength

Lastly, let's resolve to stand in God's strength, not our own. Paul wrote in Ephesians 6, "Finally, my brethren, be strong in the Lord and in the power of His might" (verse 10). This literally could be translated, "strengthen yourselves in the Lord." You don't want to mess with Satan on your own.

When the police are called to a situation more intense than they originally anticipated, what do they do? They call for backup. We need to do the same.

It reminds me of a time when I was a young boy living in New Jersey. I was walking down the street one day, wearing a cowboy hat and shooting my little cap pistols. I was thoroughly enjoying myself until some hoodlums, with names like Vinnie, came walking up to me and started pushing me around. These boys grabbed my cap pistols and pushed me to the ground. Then they walked away, laughing.

I went home and found my brother, Doug, who was five years older and a lot bigger. Doug and I went back to look for those guys, and we found them. And guess what? I was much braver than before.

I walked up to them and demanded my pistols back. Then I followed up with a shove.

They didn't lay a finger on me because my brother was behind me. They knew if they touched me, they would have to face him.

That is how it works in spiritual battle. In our own strength, we are weak. But if we stand in the Lord and in the power of His might, it is a different thing altogether. That is how we can prevail in spiritual battle.

The chief aim of Satan is to separate you from God through sin. He wants to separate our hearts from God and inspire us to put confidence in ourselves instead. He wants us to say, "Lord, don't worry. I have this one."

No, we don't. We don't have this one. In fact, we don't have anything. We need God. And we need to pray every day, "God, help me."

The good news is that God never will give us more than you can handle. The Bible says, "The temptations in your life are no different from what others experience. And God is faithful. He will not allow the temptation to be more than you can stand. When you are tempted, he will show you a way out so that you can endure" (1 Corinthians 10:13 NLT). We all face temptation. But remember this—God will not give you more than you can handle. There is always a way out of every temptation. There is always a door, there is always an off button, there is always a way out—if you look for it.

But if you are not looking for it and fall into temptation, don't say it is God's fault. You did that to yourself. God never will give you more than you can handle.

James 4:7 says, "Submit to God. Resist the devil and he will flee from you." Notice it doesn't say that if you resist the Devil, he will walk away from you. Rather, it says that he will *flee from* you. A literal translation would be, "Resist the devil and he will run away from you."

When temptation comes knocking on the door of your imagination, don't entertain it. Don't invite it in for coffee. Don't even engage it. Reject it outright.

You can even say, "Lord, I'm sorry I thought that. I repent of that. That was a sin." That way, you just closed the door on temptation.

When you let temptation in, ponder it, and contemplate it, that is when the problems begin. Flee temptation, and don't leave a forwarding address. Run from it. Keep your distance from it.

You can't do this on your own, but you can do it in the strength of Christ. That is the only way to do it. Jesus said,

> "My sheep recognize my voice. I know them, and they follow me. I give them real and eternal life. They are protected from the Destroyer for good. No one can steal them from out of my hand. The Father who put them under my care is so much greater than the Destroyer and Thief. No one could ever get them away from him. I and the Father are one heart and mind." (John 10:27–30 msg)

The Devil would like to come and rip you out of the hand of Jesus Christ. But he can't. You are under divine protection.

Paul reminds us in Romans 8, "For I am persuaded that neither death nor life, nor angels nor principalities nor powers, nor things present nor things to come, nor height nor depth, nor any other created thing, shall be able to separate us from the love of God which is in Christ Jesus our Lord" (verses 38–39).

Nothing can separate you from Him.

The Devil doesn't want you to know he was soundly defeated at the cross. As 1 John 3:8 tells us, "For this purpose the Son of God was manifested, that He might destroy the works of the devil."

As Jesus hung on the cross, He cried out *tetelestai*, a word used in that culture to declare that a project was finished. When you would prepare a nice meal and it was ready to serve, you would say, "*Tetelestai.*" If you were building a table and finally completed it, you would say, "*Tetelestai.*"

Jesus died on the cross. He absorbed the wrath of God. He paid for the sin of the world. And He said, "*Tetelestai!*" Or, as it is translated, "It is finished!" (John 19:30).

Those words reverberated through the corridors of hell as well as the hallways of Heaven. Jesus had met the righteous demands of God and had defeated Satan there. Colossians 2:14 says He "canceled the charge of our legal indebtedness, which stood against us and condemned us; he has taken it away, nailing it to the cross" (NIV). This is basically speaking of the Ten Commandments that we all have broken. Jesus wiped out the charges against us. He nailed them to the cross. The next verse continues, "And having disarmed the powers and authorities, he made a public spectacle of them, triumphing over them by the cross" (verse 15 NIV). That means believers are not fighting to obtain victory. Rather, we are resting in the victory Christ has obtained. We are not fighting *for* victory; we are fighting *from* victory. There is a big difference.

It is finished. It is accomplished. It is done. It is paid for.

We are accepted in the Beloved. We are loved by God. We have His righteousness in our lives.

THE BATTLE IS THE LORD'S

Remember, this is the Lord's battle, not yours. This is a battle between God and Satan and between light and darkness. Through Jesus Christ you will be protected. You will be kept safe. Just make sure you do your part, which is to stay as close to Him as you possibly can.

Stand in the Lord and in the power of His might.

15

WAKE UP, SOBER UP, SUIT UP

Therefore you must wear the whole armour of God that you may be able to resist evil in its day of power, and that even when you have fought to a standstill you may still stand your ground.(Ephesians 6:13 ph)

Mike Tyson once said, "Everyone has a plan until they get hit."[1] For Christians in the spiritual battle, it comes down to a choice of fighting or not fighting. We really have no other options. It is a choice of victory or defeat, a choice of winning or losing. And sometimes we can feel a little overwhelmed.

Maybe you've been getting hit a lot lately. Maybe it seems as though everywhere you turn, the Devil is up to something. He's wreaking havoc in the lives of countless people, yet he still manages to find time in his busy schedule to tempt little ol' you.

Why does he spend so much time trying to ruin lives?

The Devil is actively involved in the world today because he believes something that has an impact on what he does. He believes that Jesus Christ is coming back again. (Even though some liberal theologians don't.)

For Christians, that is good news. But for the Devil, that is really bad news. Revelation 12 says, "Therefore rejoice, you heavens and you who dwell in them! But woe to the earth and the sea, because the devil has gone down to you! He is filled with fury, because he knows that his time is short" (verse 12 NIV).

Why is he filled with fury? Because he knows his time is short. He knows his days are numbered.

Knowing time is short is an incentive for us as followers of Jesus to share our faith and live godly lives. But for the Devil, it's an incentive to attack our faith and try to make us stumble and fall. Satan basically wants to take down as many people as possible.

Most people want to make amends if they know their life will end soon. They make peace with people they have been in conflict with. The Devil is the very opposite. Knowing an end is coming to his reign, he wants to bring misery to people.

In the previous chapter, I mentioned a time in Jesus' ministry where two demon-possessed men shouted at Him, "Why are you interfering with us, Son of God? Have you come here to torture us before God's appointed time?" (Matthew 8:29 NLT). The demons know they have an appointed time. The Devil knows his day is coming, and he clearly well knows he will get his due.

WAKE UP

The terrorism, violence, and upheaval in our world and our nation that seems to get worse by the day should serve as a massive wake-up call for Christians. What we are realizing is there are no longer any social advantages to being a Christian.

Cultural Christianity is dead. That is good and bad. There are some positive aspects of cultural Christianity, such as a Judeo-Christian worldview. There was a time in our country when we were much closer to that than we are now. But we have entered a whole new phase of American history. I think the June 26, 2015, Supreme Court ruling on same-sex marriage is a real marker of time that we will remember in so many ways. We can see the trajectory our nation is on. Could God change the course of the United States? Could we go back to Him again?

Yes, I believe we could—if a revival broke out. But if there is not a revival, then I don't see anything that would stop us in the downward spiral we're in right now.

I am a child of revival. I came to put my faith in Jesus Christ during a time known as the Jesus Movement in the late '60s and early '70s. Thousands and thousands of other young people came to Christ in that time that is now regarded as the last great spiritual awakening in the United States. But that was over 40 years ago. Could it happen again? Could there be another "Jesus Revolution" as it was also called?

I believe there could.

But we need to be desperate for it.

How desperate are you to see a revival in America again?

Revival is a sovereign work that God decides to do where and when He chooses.

Having said that, we need to begin praying and preparing the ground for this awakening.

Or should I say, we need to "pre-prayer" the ground.

What are we Christians supposed to do? Paul gives us the answer: "So then, let us not be like others, who are asleep, but let us be awake and sober. For those who sleep, sleep at night, and those who get drunk, get drunk at night. But since we belong to the day, let us be sober, putting on faith and love as a breast-plate, and the hope of salvation as a helmet" (1 Thessalonians 5:6–8 NIV).

As I've already pointed out, we need to wake up. But there are two other things we must do. We must sober up. And we must suit up.

SOBER UP

In this spiritual battle, we face a formidable foe. Martin Luther wrote in "A Mighty Fortress Is Our God," a great hymn of the church,

> For still our ancient foe
>
> Doth seek to work us woe—
>
> His craft and pow'r are great,
>
> And, armed with cruel hate,
>
> On earth is not his equal.

Luther was talking about the Devil. Of course, he also said,

> A mighty fortress is our God,
>
> A bulwark never failing. . . .

The good news is this: "He who is in you is greater than he who is in the world" (1 John 4:4).

We are in a battle. And when we look at our opponent on the other side of the field, maybe we wonder how we can win this conflict. Corrie ten Boom pointed out, "The first step on the way to victory is to recognize the Enemy."[2]

Robert Greene, in his book *The 33 Strategies of War*, wrote, "You cannot fight effectively unless you can identify your enemies."[3] We must do the same.

You have heard the adages "What you don't know won't hurt you" and "Ignorance is bliss."

Not really. What you don't know *can* hurt you. And ignorance is . . . well, ignorance. Paul wrote in 2 Corinthians, "And when I forgive whatever needs to be forgiven, I do so with Christ's authority for your benefit, so that Satan will not outsmart us. For we are familiar with his evil schemes" (2:10–11 NLT). To be forewarned is to be forearmed. Our adversary, the Devil, has a lot of strategies. Sometimes he will appear as a dangerous wolf. Other times he will come as a snake. Sometimes he roars like a lion. Other times he comes as a beautiful angel.

As a kid, I loved animals of all kinds, from rabbits to Guinea pigs to parrots to dogs.

I especially loved all reptiles in general, but I especially loved snakes. At one point, I had quite an extensive snake collection. Every kind of snake you could think of, I had. I absolutely was fixated on snakes. For a time, I was even thinking of becoming a herpetologist. I would read about snakes. I would carry my snakes around. And I would look forward to the next snake I was going to get.

I don't know why my mother put up with this madness, but she did, for the most part. There was one day, however, when one of the snakes got out of its cage when I was at school. As Mom watched it slither toward the sliding glass door, she simply walked over, opened the door, and let it go. It happened to be my favorite snake.

There was at least one advantage to having snakes, though. I got a car out of it. My mom drove a classic baby blue Ford Starliner, one of those big cars from the early 1960s. One day, we went to pick up a snake at a pet shop in Costa Mesa. I put the snake in a little cage in the trunk of the Starliner, and we drove home. But when I opened the trunk to retrieve my snake, he was gone. That meant he was loose somewhere in the car.

My mom didn't drive that car for about two months, but finally she had to. As she waited at an intersection for the light to change, she felt a cold coil suddenly drop on her ankle. She jumped out of the car, screaming. There happened to be a police officer nearby who ran up to find out what was wrong. When he looked inside the car, he discovered it was a loose hose that had dropped on her ankle.

My mom never drove that car again. She told me, "You can have it."

So that's one way to get your parent's car I suppose.

One thing I learned about snakes is that you never know where you stand with them. Unlike dogs, which are easy to read, you don't know what a snake is thinking. He could be looking at you and thinking, *I love you.* (Although I doubt a cold-blooded reptile has such thoughts.) Or, he might be thinking, *I'm going to bite you in the face right now.* Another thing about snakes is that if you give them a little bit of space, they will get out of their cage.

The Bible refers to the Devil as a snake, or a serpent on more than one occasion. And just like a snake, if you give the Devil an inch, he will take a mile. If you give him just a little, he will take a whole lot more. You can't mess around with him. Sometimes he will come in all of his depravity. And other times, as I've said, he will come as an angel of light.

Stand in God's Strength

In Ephesians 6, before a word is mentioned about what pieces of armor to put on, Paul tells us, "Finally, my brethren, be strong in the Lord and in the power of His might" (verse 10). We need to stand in God's strength, not our own.

You and I are no match for the Devil. We don't want to take him on in our own strength. We want to stay as close to Jesus as we possibly can and rest in Him, remembering that Christ already has dealt the decisive blow against the Devil and his demons. At the cross of Calvary, He cried out, "It is finished!" We rest in the work that He did. As I pointed out earlier, we don't fight to get victory. We fight because we *have* victory. We don't fight for victory; we fight *from* victory.

It is a good thing to have a healthy respect for our adversary. I cringe when I hear preachers calling the Devil silly names and mocking him. Don't mess around with Satan. Jude tells us, "Yet Michael the archangel, in contending with the devil, when he disputed about the body of Moses, dared not bring against him a reviling accusation, but said, 'The Lord rebuke you!'" (verse 9) Michael, a powerful angel whose power certainly would be equal to the power of Satan (and arguably more powerful because we read in Daniel that he overcame him) wouldn't even dare condemn him with mockery. Michael simply said, "The Lord rebuke you."

I want to have as little to do with Satan as possible. I certainly don't want to have extended conversations with him. I simply want to say, "The Lord rebuke you" and get on with my business. I want to stay close to Jesus Christ, because that is my power base.

Satan wants to separate us from that power base. That is why he tries to talk us out of going to church, interrupts when we are having a Bible study, and tries to distract us from praying. He doesn't want us to pray. He doesn't want us to study the Scriptures. He doesn't want us to be with God's people. And when we go out of our way to do those things, it drives him crazy. It also makes us stronger Christians.

Psalm 91 says, "He who dwells in the secret place of the Most High shall abide under the shadow of the Almighty. I will say of the Lord, 'He is my refuge and my fortress; My God, in Him I will trust'" (verses 1–2) Stay close to Him.

Jesus said, "Abide in Me, and I in you. As the branch cannot bear fruit of itself, unless it abides in the vine, neither can you, unless you abide in Me" (John 15:4). To abide in Christ means to sink your roots deeply into Him, maintaining communion with Him, and growing closer to Him each day. "He who abides in Me," Jesus said, "brings forth much fruit" (verse 5). That is the best place to be.

Notice there is a specific order to Paul's instructions in Ephesians 6:10–11: "A final word: Be strong in the Lord and in his mighty power. Put on all of God's armor so that you will be able to stand firm against all strategies of the devil" (NLT). Paul doesn't tell us to put on the armor and be strong in the Lord. He tells us to be strong in the Lord and put on the armor.

If a soldier didn't have the physique to support his armor, he wouldn't be able to do much. Then again, if he had an impressive physique but didn't arm himself, he would be vulnerable. That's why we need to first be strong in the Lord.

SUIT UP

To make his point, Paul referred to the various pieces of armor that a Roman soldier would wear. Don't forget that Paul spent a great deal of time in prison. Sometimes he was in a dungeon. At other times he was under house arrest.

Paul would have had guards close by, perhaps a centurion, or perhaps a common Roman soldier. He also would have had a lot of time to converse with them. We know that Paul led some of them to Christ, because in one of his epistles, he sends greetings from "those who are of Caesar's household" (Philippians 4:22). Some in Caesar's palace no doubt came to Christ through the testimony of Paul.

The point is that he probably would sit around and talk with them. I can imagine Paul saying, "Tell me how all of this equipment functions. How does the helmet work? What is the objective of the breastplate? How is one to utilize the sword for maximum benefit?"

As a result of these conversations, I have no doubt Paul had an operative understanding of how Roman armor worked. And he used that as a picture of how we are to put on the armor of God.

Every piece of armor is important. Every piece is interconnected. Every piece must be used.

As I mentioned earlier, when Paul wrote, "Put on the whole armor of God," it carried the meaning of doing this once and for all. It's not as though we put it on in the morning and then peel it off at night. We keep it on all the time.

The idea is to always keep your guard up. You never know when you will come under spiritual attack. There is no such thing as a spiritual vacation.

I actually met someone once who said he was on a spiritual vacation. I was with my family at a mall, and he walked up to me and asked if I was Greg Laurie. We started talking, and I asked him where he went to church.

He said, "I'm sort of on a spiritual vacation."

"What on earth is that?"

"I'm just taking a vacation from God and Bible study and my Christian life," he said. "I'm just doing other things. I'm going to end my vacation eventually and recommit my life to the Lord."

I told him that was the craziest thing I had ever heard. We talked for a while, and fortunately, he prayed and made a recommitment to Christ that day.

We can't take a spiritual vacation. If we take time off from our walk with God, we will fall away. If you don't go to church for a month, the odds are almost two to one that you won't go for more than a year.

Paul learned about all of this armor and wanted to explain it to us. However, we can't pick and choose what piece of armor appeals to us personally. We need to use all of it. This armor speaks of what God has done for us and what we should do for God. This armor shows what God has given us and what our appropriate response should be to that. We put on all of the armor of God. If we leave one piece out, that will be the area where we're vulnerable.

We might think we're strong in a certain area of our lives. We may think we'll never fall in that regard—ever. But the very area in which we think we are the strongest may be the very area in which we have a lapse or weakness. The Bible warns us, "If you think you are standing firm, be careful that you don't fall!" (1 Corinthians 10:12 NIV). It also tells us that "pride goes before destruction, and a haughty spirit before a fall" (Proverbs 16:18).

It is interesting to note that many of the great people in the Bible fell in the very area that was supposedly their greatest strength. We think of Abraham as a man of faith and rightly so. Yet, as we read his story, we see that he had serious lapses of faith. On one occasion, he asked his beautiful wife Sarah to pose as his sister. He thought if King Abimelech found out she was his wife, he would kill Abraham and take her away. Abraham had lapses of faith. He was weak in an area in which we know he was ultimately strong.

The Bible tells us that Moses was the meekest man on the face of the earth, yet he lost his temper on one occasion, and it kept him out of the Promised Land. Granted, he put up with a lot. But one day, the people were complaining because there wasn't any water. Moses prayed, and the Lord told him, "Take the rod; you and your brother Aaron gather the congregation together. Speak to the rock before their eyes, and it will yield its water; thus you shall bring water for them out of the rock, and give drink to the congregation and their animals" (Numbers 20:8).

Moses walked over to the rock with his rod and said, "Hear now, you rebels! Must we bring water for you out of this rock?" (verse 10).

Water rushed out, and everyone was happy. But God said to Moses and Aaron, "Because you did not trust in me enough to honor me as holy in the sight of the Israelites, you will not bring this community into the land I give them" (verse 12 NIV). Moses had a lapse in his meekness. The very area in which he was thought to be strong was the area in which he showed weakness.

Simon Peter certainly was a courageous man. Church tradition tells us that he was crucified upside down. He also was one of the first to volunteer to become a follower of Jesus Christ. When Jesus dropped the bombshell that He was going to be betrayed, it was Peter who said, "Even if all are made to stumble, yet I will not be" (Mark 14:29).

Then Jesus said, "Today, even this night, before the rooster crows twice, you will deny Me three times" (verse 30).

Still, Peter had the audacity to essentially say, "Sorry, Jesus. You're wrong on that one. That's not going to happen. Though all deny You, I never will deny you."

We know the rest of that story. He did exactly what Jesus said he would do.

Abraham, Moses, and Simon Peter all fell in areas where they never thought they would fall. Their examples should serve as a warning to us. Let's not become self-confident. We need the whole armor of God.

The Belt of Truth

Let's look at the first piece of armor, the utility belt of truth: "Stand therefore, having girded your waist with truth" (Ephesians 6:14 NLT). A Roman soldier wore a large belt, which was key to the entire apparatus of his armor. His breastplate was attached to the belt. His sword was attached to the belt. When he went into battle, he would use the belt to cinch up his long, flowing robe so he would have freedom of movement.

There are a few things this belt speaks of. The first is readiness. Paul was saying, "Gird your waist with truth." The term *gird* is used elsewhere in the Bible. Moses told the Israelites, "And thus shall ye eat [the Passover meal]; with your loins girded, your shoes on your feet, and your staff in your hand; and ye shall eat it in haste: it is the Lord's passover" (Exodus 12:11 kjv). *Gird* speaks of readiness.

Jesus, speaking of His return, said, "Let your waist be girded and your lamps burning" (Luke 12:35). If we were to put this in the modern vernacular, it would be like saying, "Have your car filled up with gas, have your cell phone charged, and be dressed and ready to go."

You want to be ready. That is the idea here. Put on the belt of truth. Be in a state of readiness.

Police officers wear a utility belt called a Sam Brown. It isn't a belt to hold their pants up. Rather, it holds all their police equipment. It has a holster for their gun, a place for their handcuffs, and a place for some pepper spray. Maybe it has a little holder for a doughnut, even. Without a Sam Brown, a police officer is in serious trouble. All of his or her gear is on the Sam Brown.

If a Roman soldier took off his belt, his clothing would drop down. His sword would drop to the ground. His breastplate would drop off. He would be vulnerable.

Though it isn't as exciting as a breastplate or a sword, a belt is essential. Without his belt, a soldier isn't going anywhere.

The utility belt of truth also represents a life and mind that are pulled together and ready to serve for the glory of God. That starts with the truth of what the Bible says about everything. Far too often, we don't think biblically. A follower of Jesus Christ needs a good working knowledge of the Scriptures. One of the signs of the end times is that "some will depart from the faith, giving heed to deceiving spirits and doctrines of demons" (1 Timothy 4:1).

How will we know right from wrong and true from false if we don't have a working knowledge of the Scriptures? I think our culture, more than any other, is being led by their feelings. People emote. They feel. But Christians need to think. God says, "Come now, and let us reason together" (Isaiah 1:18).

I didn't really start thinking until I became a Christian. I marched in lockstep with everyone else in my culture. But after I became a believer, I really started thinking for myself.

I find it funny that non-Christians say, "Christians are all brainwashed. They're like automatons."

It's actually the opposite. Non-Christians are that way. It's almost as though they walk around saying, "What is the latest trend? What is the cool thing? That is what we believe. That is what we think."

The belt of truth also refers to truth in our heart of hearts. David said of God, "Behold, You desire truth in the inward parts, and in the hidden part You will make me to know wisdom" (Psalm 51:6). To wear the belt of truth means that as a Christian, you live a sincere, honest, candid life before God and others. It is a life devoid of secrets, ongoing sin, and duplicity. Some people try to live that way. They want to live in both worlds. But it doesn't work that way.

When you join the Lord's army, you are there to stay. As Paul wrote to Timothy, "No one engaged in warfare entangles himself with the affairs of this life, that he may please him who enlisted him as a soldier" (2 Timothy 2:4). We are in a war. We cannot entangle ourselves with other things. We're soldiers. We're in a battle. Duplicity and hypocrisy weaken any witness we have before a watching world.

It especially weakens our witness in our own families. The worst thing parents can do is be hypocritical in the home. I am not saying parents have to be perfect; no parent is—present company included. But probably all parents should get around to apologizing to their children at some point. It doesn't diminish a parent's authority to tell a child, "I'm sorry. I shouldn't have said that. I shouldn't have done that." It actually will make your child respect you more and go a long way to restore communication between you and the ones you love.

I think we're hypocrites in our homes if we say one thing to everyone else and then contradict it in the way we live. We're basically showing our kids that our faith is worthless. I feel sorry for kids who were raised in homes where their parents were hypocrites or where their parents divorced with no biblical grounds for it. We need to stop and think about the impact these things have on non-Christians who are watching our lives.

Remember, Satan is a liar. In fact, he is the father of lies. When he lies to us, we must refute him with God's truth. When he prompts us to make bad choices, we must make wise choices instead. When he tempts us, we must stand firm. When he promises instant gratification, we must rest on the truth of God's Word. That is girding up the belt of truth.

The Breastplate of Righteousness

Next we come to the breastplate of righteousness. You probably have seen enough Roman soldiers in movies to know what a breastplate is. It usually was made of leather or metal and was shaped to the torso of the soldier. It was an essential piece of armor. No Roman soldier would go into battle without his breastplate on. It protected his vital organs.

Our modern equivalent would be wearing a bulletproof vest. Some guys I know in law enforcement have said they don't particularly like to wear bulletproof vests because they're hot. They're thick. They're uncomfortable. But they can potentially stop a lot of bullets. Police officers wouldn't go on duty without a gun. And if they're in uniform, they need to wear their vest as well because they're targets.

In the same way, we are always on duty as Christians. We have to keep the breastplate of righteousness on. The Bible says, "Be prepared in season and out of season" (2 Timothy 4:2 NIV). The breastplate of righteous refers to the righteousness given to us by Jesus Christ. Remember, the first part of Ephesians talks about the amazing things God has done for us and all of the riches we have in Christ. He chose us. He saved us. He justified us. He adopted us. He put the righteousness of Jesus Christ into our spiritual bank account, which is called the imputed righteousness of Christ (see Philippians 3:9). When you believe in Jesus, you become a righteous person. It is not based on what you have done for God but on what God has done for you.

We put on a breastplate of righteousness, not a breastplate of *self-righteousness*. That wouldn't protect you; it would mislead you. It would be like going into a battle wearing plastic armor or trying to fight a gun battle with a toy gun.

This is one of the Devil's most effective tactics he uses in a Christian's life. He doesn't want us to know that we have the righteousness of Christ in our account. He doesn't want us to know that we are justified before God.

Let's say, for example, that the Devil comes along and tempts you. He lays out all his enticements. First he says, "Why don't you go ahead and commit this sin? You'll get away with it. No one will ever know. I won't tell if you won't."

Maybe he gets you to take a nibble. And then finally you take the bait. You go down that road with him.

He immediately says, "What a pathetic hypocrite you are! You call yourself a Christian after what you just did? You're the worst hypocrite ever!"

You start to believe it.

"You can't go to God," he tells you. "You can't pray. You can't read the Bible." He condemns you and drives you away.

The Bible calls Satan "the accuser of our brothers and sisters, who accuses them before our God day and night" (Revelation 12:10 niv). He hits us with the double whammy of accusation and condemnation. We need real righteousness. Earlier in Ephesians, we learned that God the Father "predestined us to adoption as sons by Jesus Christ to Himself, according to the good pleasure of His will, to the praise of the glory of His grace, by which He made us accepted in the Beloved" (1:5–6). That is imputed righteousness. As Christians, we stand righteous before Jesus Christ.

Having said that, it doesn't mean we should say, "That's great! I can just go out and sin up a storm, and still I'm righteous before God."

Careful. You're missing the point. There is practical righteousness, which should come as a result of imputed righteousness. After God has done something so wonderful for us, we want to do something in return—not to earn what He has given, but to express our gratitude. This should motivate us to cast off sinful behavior and live godly lives.

Paul summed this up perfectly when he wrote, "Run from anything that stimulates youthful lusts. Instead, pursue righteous living, faithfulness, love, and peace. Enjoy the companionship of those who call on the Lord with pure hearts" (2 Timothy 2:22 NLT). Show me your friends, and I will show you your future. Who do you hang out with? They will have an influence on you. Who hangs out with you? You will have an influence on them. If you're around ungodly people all the time, and you find they are pulling you down, it shouldn't surprise you. On the other hand, if you are with godly people and are chasing after the things of God, that will impact you as well.

We see an excellent picture of this in Psalm 1:

Blessed is the man

Who walks not in the counsel of the ungodly,

Nor stands in the path of sinners,

Nor sits in the seat of the scornful;

But his delight is in the law of the Lord,

And in His law he meditates day and night.

He shall be like a tree

Planted by the rivers of water,

That brings forth its fruit in its season,

Whose leaf also shall not wither;

And whatever he does shall prosper. (verses 1–3)

The word *blessed* could be translated "happy." Notice the man of Psalm 1 (and this applies to women too) does certain things and does not do other things. If you want to be a happy person, don't walk in the counsel of the ungodly. Don't stand in the way of sinners. Don't sit in the seat of the scornful. Instead, let your delight be in the law of the Lord (or the Word of God). Meditate in it day and night.

As a Christian, there are certain things you shouldn't do. There are certain things you should do.

It's like trying to lose weight. It's a matter of doing a combination of things. You have to think about what you eat. You have to increase your activity. There are certain things you shouldn't do, and there are certain things you should do.

The same is true of the Christian life. Think about what you put in your system. Be active in serving the Lord and walking with Him.

Put on the breastplate of righteousness. Stand in the righteousness of Christ. Then let that motivate you to live a righteous life.

The Shoes of the Gospel of Peace

Next, we arm ourselves by having our "feet fitted with the readiness that comes from the gospel of peace" (Ephesians 6:15 NIV). Roman soldiers would wear boots all the way up to their knees as well as guards on their legs to protect against the enemy's blows. The boots would give them firm footedness as they walked.

Today we have different kinds of shoes for different occasions. We have dress shoes. We have workout shoes. But we need the right shoe for the right activity.

Having our "feet fitted with the readiness that comes from the gospel of peace" is how we advance. What do we do with our feet? We walk forward with them. And the way we gain ground in the spiritual battle is through the proclamation of the gospel. In Romans we read,

> But how can they call on him to save them unless they believe in him? And how can they believe in him if they have never heard about him? And how can they hear about him unless someone tells them? And how will anyone go and tell them without being sent? That is why the Scriptures say, "How beautiful are the feet of messengers who bring good news!" (10:14–15 NLT)

Look at your feet right now. Are they beautiful?

Well, after my pedicure they will be.

I don't mean that kind of beauty. If you are using your life to bring the gospel to others, that means you have beautiful feet. But know this: As you seek to gain ground in the spiritual battle, don't expect a standing ovation from hell. Expect opposition. Satan hates evangelism. Perhaps the reason so many Christians are immobilized in this area is because the Devil defeats them before they ever get started.

We must have all the pieces of God's armor in place, and that includes what goes on our feet. Put on the shoes of "readiness that comes from the gospel of peace."

The Shield of Faith

Next Paul said, "In addition to all of these, hold up the shield of faith to stop the fiery arrows of the devil" (Ephesians 6:16 NIV). The shield was used for close combat. It obviously was very large, possibly covering most of the person. Interestingly, these shields were coated with some type of fire repellent. One of the tactics of first-century warfare was firing a barrage of flaming arrows at the enemy. Thus, a soldier would put up his shield to protect himself from those flaming arrows.

We need to take up the shield of faith in the spiritual battle. Flaming arrows will come our way, swiftly and silently. Rarely do we receive an advance warning about them. We can simply wake up in the morning and be hit with a fiery dart from the Enemy.

Has that ever happened to you? You're just rubbing the sleep out of your eyes and are suddenly hit with an impure thought or a feeling of complete despair. You might find yourself gripped with intense fear or terror as you're thinking, *What if this happens? What if that happens?* Maybe it's a thought of hatred toward someone. It even could be a blasphemous thought against God.

You think, *Where is that coming from?*

That was a flaming arrow directed at you.

You need to get out the shield of faith, hold it up, and defend yourself. Deflect those arrows when they come your way.

Holding up the shield of faith means that we stand in the promises of God. Stand on what God has told us in His Word. He has made specific promises that will help us when we're being attacked. We do not stand on our fluctuating feelings but rather on the solid foundation of God's Word to us.

Someone has estimated there are eight thousand promises for the believer in the Bible. We are to take hold of the promises of God. But this requires a working knowledge of the Scriptures and understanding what the Bible says.

Maybe the Enemy says, *You're not going to make it. You're not going to survive as a Christian.*

You can quote Philippians 1:6: "Being confident of this very thing, that He who has begun a good work in you will complete it until the day of Jesus Christ." And Hebrews 12:2 says that Jesus is "the author and finisher of our faith."

Maybe you're in need financially, and the Devil says, *You're never going to get through this.*

Lay hold of Philippians 4:19: "And my God shall supply all your need according to His riches in glory by Christ Jesus."

Or the Devil says, *You're going to be destroyed.*

Turn to Psalm 91, which promises God's protection.

When the lies come, the shield goes up. Again, the Bible does not tell us to stand firm in our feelings; it tells us to stand firm in our faith (see 1 Peter 5:9).

The Roman soldiers also would use their shields in an effective defensive maneuver. To protect themselves from a barrage of arrows, they would lock their shields together above their heads and to their sides, effectively forming a box to deflect them. Then the soldiers would break and attack again.

It's very important for us to know that we are not alone in this spiritual battle. We have fellow soldiers marching with us, and we can do a lot more together than we can apart. That is one of the reasons the Devil tries to divide believers. We want to stand together, pray together, and march together. That will help us effectively defend ourselves when attacks come.

During World War II, Claire Chennault led a group of pilots known as the Flying Tigers, credited with downing 296 enemy aircraft. Their secret was *cooperation*. Even if they were outnumbered ten to one, the Flying Tigers always attacked two at a time.

There is a scriptural principle for us in their strategy. Jesus said, "I say to you that if two of you agree on earth concerning anything that they ask, it will be done for them by My Father in heaven" (Matthew 18:19).

Jesus called His twelve disciples together and then "began to send them out two by two, and gave them power over unclean spirits" (Mark 6:7). We are stronger together than we are alone.

None of us will make it as a solo Christian. One of the first things someone said to me as a young Christian was that being in fellowship with other believers is like a lot of burning coals. If you take one coal from the others, it will soon cool down. But if you keep it next to the others, all the coals will keep burning.

Hebrews 10:25 tells us, "And let us not neglect our meeting together, as some people do, but encourage one another, especially now that the day of his return is drawing near" (NLT). Instead of spending so much time arguing or dividing over theological minutiae, Christians should try to discover what we have in common, march together, and love one another.

This is a global fight. The church all around the world is under attack. Right now, in places like the Middle East, our brothers and sisters in Christ are facing severe persecution at the hands of Muslim extremists. Others live under oppressive Communist rule. Christians are suffering around the world. Rather than face these attacks on our own, we need to pray for one another.

As 1 Peter 5 warns us, "Stay alert! Watch out for your great enemy, the devil. He prowls around like a roaring lion, looking for someone to devour. Stand firm against him, and be strong in your faith. Remember that your family of believers all over the world is going through the same kind of suffering you are" (verses 8–9 NLT).

Let's take up the shield of faith—together.

The Helmet of Salvation

Then Paul tells us to "take the helmet of salvation" (Ephesians 6:17). A Roman soldier's helmet could take a crushing blow and protect him in battle. Even if his helmet was damaged, he could still march forward. But without his helmet, he was very vulnerable.

For the Christian, the helmet of salvation speaks of protecting our minds. The mind is command central. If we were to retrace our steps whenever we give in to a temptation, we would discover that it started in our minds.

The Devil comes with a thought like this: *I know you would never do this because you are so wonderful and righteous and holy, and you love Jesus so much. But just for fun, why don't you take this little thought for a test drive? Why don't you have just a little nibble of this? Just play with it a little.*

Satan recognizes the value of first getting a foothold in the realm of our thoughts and imagination because it will prepare the way for those thoughts to translate into action. This is why he will hit us first in our minds.

The Pharisees smugly thought because they didn't technically commit adultery they were free of sin. But Jesus said to them, "Anyone who even looks at a woman with lust has already committed adultery with her in his heart" (Matthew 5:28 NLT). He was pointing out that just because you don't do something doesn't mean you aren't doing it in your mind. That, too, is a sin.

We want to nip sin in the bud. It isn't enough not to do something outwardly. We don't want to do it in our mind, heart, or imagination, either. This is important because there may come a moment in your life when you feel as though you might get away with a certain sin. You might try to do it. But what stops you from doing that horrible thing? It's the fear of being found out.

When the day comes that you think you can get away with something, you will want to do it. But if you can win the battle in your mind when that "opportunity" comes along, you won't do it. That is because it is no longer just the fear of being caught that prevents you from sinning. It's also the fear of offending God.

When Joseph was tempted by Potiphar's wife, he responded, "How then can I do this great wickedness, and sin against God?" (Genesis 39:9). I love that. There was no one around to see. He could have justified it by saying it would advance his career. But he said, in effect, "God is watching, and I won't do it." That is the best deterrent of all.

Have you ever noticed you can't think two thoughts at the same time? In other words, you can't have a pure thought and an impure thought simultaneously. When evil thoughts come, reject them and replace them with pure thoughts.

As 2 Corinthians 10:4–5 points out, "We use our powerful God-tools for smashing warped philosophies, tearing down barriers erected against the truth of God, fitting every loose thought and emotion and impulse into the structure of life shaped by Christ" (msg). The same goes for worry. When worries come, turn them into prayers. Philippians 4:6 tells us, "Don't worry about anything; instead, pray about everything. Tell God what you need, and thank him for all he has done" (nlt). It has been more than seven years since our son Christopher died. That day was the worst day of our lives. In all honesty, I did not know if I even would survive that dark tragic day. The pain is still very strong, but we are not in the same pain we were at the beginning. Right after he died, it was very hard for me to sleep. I was barraged with horrible thoughts. I would go to sleep for a few minutes and wake up again.

The Devil would whisper in my ear, *Your life is over. You never will be happy again. You're not going to survive this.*

I had to take a disciplined approach to what I thought about. I had to take every one of those thoughts and either accept it or reject it. I set up a biblical grid in my life that I ran everything through.

When a frightening thought came, I would replace it with a biblical one.

When the Devil whispered, *You never will see him again. You never will hear his voice again,* I would respond, "That is a lie. Jesus said He is the resurrection and the life, and whoever lives and believes in Him will never die. My son will never die. I will be reunited with him. David said of his son who died, 'I shall go to him, but he shall not return to me.' The Bible says that 'we who are alive and remain shall be caught up together with them in the clouds to meet the Lord in the air.'"

When the Enemy attacks your mind, bring the Bible into play. Sentimental thoughts won't help you in a spiritual battle. That is why theology matters.

We need to be careful about what we think. Experts tell us that for each action we take, the brain creates a neurological pathway that paves the way for familiarity the next time. You take that action, and your mind will know what to do. As you continually repeat behaviors, those pathways become more stable. A simple behavior maps out a dirt road in your brain. As you repeat that behavior, your brain creates a concrete high-way of sorts. That could be good or bad, depending on your thoughts.

Train yourself to think properly. Train your mind to think biblically. We have natural reflexes and conditioned reflexes. If I touch a hot stove, I'll pull my hand away. Why? Because it hurts. I don't need an explanation. I feel pain. That is a natural reflex. A conditioned reflex is something I have learned to do, like typing on a keyboard. It took some time to learn. I have taught myself a conditioned reflex.

When bad, evil, or impure thoughts make their way into our minds, we must teach ourselves to turn them into something else. That is putting on the helmet of salvation.

The Sword of the Spirit

Now we come to the only offensive weapon Paul lists with the armor of God: "And take . . . the sword of the Spirit, which is the word of God" (Ephesians 6:17).

When a soldier goes into battle, he isn't going to throw his helmet at the enemy. He isn't going to beat the enemy to death with his utility belt or rip off his breastplate and launch it at his opponent. Instead, the soldier will use the only offensive weapon in his armor: the sword.

Paul says the sword of the Spirit is the Word of God.

There are many Christians today who have their armor in place and are wearing the shoes of the preparation of the gospel of peace. They are holding up their shield of faith. Everything is good. The problem is their sword is still in its sheath. That won't do them any good. They have to take out their sword and start using it.

The Devil doesn't want you to know how to use the sword. As I've often said of the Bible, sin will keep you from this book, and this book will keep you from sin.

It's amazing how we can watch a news program on television, look at our favorite website, update our Facebook page, post a photo on Instagram, send out four tweets, and text twenty people—and everything is quiet on the home front.

But the moment we open up the Word of God, all hell breaks loose. It isn't just the crazy things that happen, but it's also the random thoughts that jump into our mind about everything we have to do. So we go do those things, and we don't get back to the Word of God.

That is where discipline comes in. Determine to start every day with the Word of God. Make it a habit. Establish that concrete roadway in your mind. Stay with it. Don't let the enemy keep you from it.

The Devil will try to stop you from studying, knowing, and learning the Word of God.

Notice this weapon is called the sword of the Spirit. The Bible was inspired by the Holy Spirit. According to 2 Timothy 3:16, "All Scripture is given by inspiration of God." This can literally be translated, "All Scripture is breathed by God." This is God's Word to us.

The Holy Spirit will bring Scripture verses to mind in situations where we need it. Sometimes when we're sharing our faith, a verse suddenly comes to mind. Maybe you read three chapters one morning, and later that day you're having a conversation with someone. They ask you a question, and all of a sudden, you remember a verse you read that morning. You don't even remember consciously memorizing it, but you're quoting it verbatim. Then these other thoughts start coming from the Scriptures. That isn't you; that is the Holy Spirit. God is taking the Word that He inspired and is applying it to specific situations in your life, enabling you to help others.

When Jesus was tested by Satan in the wilderness, He took the Word of God and used it like a sword. Jesus had been fasting for forty days and forty nights when the Devil came to Him and said, "If You are the Son of God, command that these stones become bread" (Matthew 4:3).

Jesus answered, "It is written, 'Man shall not live by bread alone, but by every word that proceeds from the mouth of God'" (verse 4).

Then the Devil took Him to a high point of the temple and said, "If You are the Son of God, throw Yourself down. For it is written: 'He shall give His angels charge over you,' and, 'In their hands they shall bear you up, lest you dash your foot against a stone'" (verse 6). Interestingly, Satan quoted from part of Psalm 91.

Jesus responded by quoting Scripture in context: "It is written again, 'You shall not tempt the Lord your God'" (verse 7).

Jesus took the Word of God that proceeds from the mouth of God and used it like a sword. We use the sword of the Spirit to defend ourselves. But we use it offensively too.

I have a question for you: What condition is your sword in? Is it polished through daily use as you study the Scripture on a regular basis? Is it sharpened on the anvil of experience as you've applied and obeyed its truths in your life? Or, is your sword rusty from lack of preparation? Is it dulled by disobedience?

If you neglect the study of the Word of God, your spiritual life ultimately will unravel, because everything you need to know about God is found in the Bible. It is great to carry a Bible in your purse or briefcase, but the best place to carry the Word of God is in your heart. As the psalmist said, "Your word I have hidden in my heart, that I might not sin against You" (Psalm 119:11).

In Deuteronomy, God commanded the people of Israel:

> "So commit yourselves wholeheartedly to these words of mine. Tie them to your hands and wear them on your forehead as reminders. Teach them to your children. Talk about them when you are at home and when you are on the road, when you are going to bed and when you are getting up. Write them on the doorposts of your house and on your gates." (11:18–20 NLT)

I think it's helpful to write down God's Word. It's a great way to remember it. I've often found that I remember things better when I write them down. So if a verse speaks to you, underline it in your Bible. It's okay to do that. Use different colors if you want to. Write notes in the margins. It will help you remember. The Bible becomes very familiar to you that way. And once the Scriptures are ingrained in your memory, they will be there to use later in life.

When I see a beat-up Bible, I think, *There is a person who is really studying God's Word.* A Bible that is falling apart usually is an indication of a life that isn't.

Learn to use the sword of the Spirit.

THE IMPORTANCE OF PRAYER

Paul, after describing the armor of God, pulls everything together by saying,

> Pray in the Spirit at all times and on every occasion. Stay alert and be persistent in your prayers for all believers everywhere.
>
> And pray for me, too. Ask God to give me the right words so I can boldly explain God's mysterious plan that the Good News is for Jews and Gentiles alike. I am in chains now, still preaching this message as God's ambassador. So pray that I will keep on speaking boldly for him, as I should. (Ephesians 6:18–20 NLT)

The Word of God and prayer are inseparable. The leaders of the early church gave themselves "continually to prayer and to the ministry of the word" (Acts 6:4). Jesus said, "If you abide in Me, and My words abide in you, you will ask what you desire, and it shall be done for you" (John 15:7).

One of the secrets to answered prayer is knowing the Word of God. As we pray biblically and start praying for what God wants us to have, we will see our prayers answered more often in the affirmative. The Word of God enlightens us. The Word of God reveals the will of God. Prayer enables us to do the will of God. Through prayer, we can apply the Word of God. But we have to open it and read it.

This is the armor that God has given to every follower of Jesus Christ. And if you don't put on the armor of God, you have no defense against the Devil.

FIGHT TO THE FINISH

Spiritual warfare is very real. We engage in it every day. It doesn't get easier as we get older and as we grow spiritually. In fact, in some ways, the battle will intensify toward the end for those who are serving God.

I know sometimes we would like the battle to stop. We would like to just go home and take a nap. But there is no break from this battle.

Yet God has not left us defenseless. He has equipped us. He has given us armor to wear.

We do not need to be sitting ducks or mere dartboards for the Devil. There are clear steps we can take as Christians to move forward and spiritually attack in this battle. The operative word is *attack*.

We need not sit around wringing our hands over what the Devil is doing. We can employ a definite biblical strategy to take back the ground we've lost.

Let's wake up.

Let's sober up.

Let's suit up.

AFTERWORD

You don't have to be a victim in the spiritual battle anymore. You can be more than a conqueror. You can come under His protection. You can know that God has a plan and a purpose for your life.

But if you don't have this relationship with God through Jesus Christ, you are vulnerable. It is true that God loves you and has a wonderful plan for your life. But it is also true that Satan hates you and has a horrible plan for your life. You will see that in time. Don't go down that road. Don't waste your life.

Jesus Christ loved you so much that He came to this earth, He went to the cross, and He died there for your sin—and for mine. He took all of our sins upon Himself. Then He rose from the dead.

A lot of people died on crosses two thousand years ago, and Jesus was one of them. But only one died on a cross who was fully God and fully man. Only one who was fully God and fully man rose again from the dead. That was Jesus. He now stands at the door of your life, and He is knocking. He is saying that if you will hear His voice and open the door, He will come in.

Have you ever asked Jesus to forgive you of your sin? Do you have the assurance right now that if you were to die, you would go to Heaven? If you don't have it, would you like to have it? He is only a prayer away. I would like to give you an opportunity to get right with God. If you would like to have a relationship with Jesus Christ, simply pray this prayer and mean it in your heart:

> "Dear Lord Jesus, I know I am a sinner. I believe You died for my sins. Right now, I turn from my sins and open the door of my heart and life. I confess You as my personal Lord and Savior. Thank You for saving me. Amen."

If you have made a decision to follow Christ today, I would like to hear from you and send you some materials to help you grow in your relationship with Him. Please contact me at www.harvest.org.

If you have an urgent need for immediate spiritual counseling, please call 951-687-6902 from 9:00 a.m. to 5:00 p.m. Pacific time.

NOTES

CHAPTER 2: WHY GOD CHOSE YOU

1. Quoted in George Sweeting, *Who Said That?: More than 2,500 Usable Quotes and Illustrations* (Chicago: Moody Publishers, 1995), Kindle edition.

2. C. H. Spurgeon, "The Immutability of God," The Spurgeon Archive, http://www.spurgeon.org/sermons/0001.htm/.

3. Quoted in Warren Wiersbe, *Be Rich: Gaining the Things That Money Can't Buy* (Colorado Springs, CO: David C. Cook, 2010), 34.

CHAPTER 5: PREPARED FOR GOOD WORKS

1. Timothy Keller, *The Obedient Master* (New York: Dutton, 2013), PDF e-book.

CHAPTER 7: AT HOME IN YOUR HEART

1. C. S. Lewis, *Mere Christianity* (New York: HarperCollins, 2015), 134.

CHAPTER 8: WALKING LESSONS

1. *Taken*, directed by Pierre Morel (2008; Los Angeles, CA: Twentieth Century Fox, 2009), DVD.

2. Friedrich Nietzsche, *Beyond Good and Evil: Prelude to a Philosophy of the Future*, trans. Helen Zimmern (New York: Macmillan, 1907), 107.

CHAPTER 10: THINGS THAT SADDEN GOD

1. Quoted in C. Douglas Weaver, ed., *From Our Christian Heritage: Hundreds of Ways to Add Christian History to Teaching, Preaching, and Writing* (Macon, GA: Smyth & Helwys Publishing, 1997), 55.

CHAPTER 12: GOD'S PLAN FOR SEX AND MARRIAGE

1. Katrina Trinko, "The Road to Forever: Hilary Duff's Marriage Miscue," *New York Post*, March 6, 2015, http://nypost.com/2015/03/06/the-road-to-forever-hilary-duffs-marriage-miscue/.

2. Quoted in M. L. Weems, *The Life of George Washington: With Curious Anecdotes, Equally Honourable to Himself, and Exemplary to His Young Countrymen* (Philadelphia: Joseph Allen, 1837), 184.

3. Timothy Keller, with Kathy Keller, *The Meaning of Marriage: Facing the Complexities of Commitment with the Wisdom of God* (New York: Dutton, 2013), 6.

4. 4C. S. Lewis, *Mere Christianity*, in *The Complete C. S. Lewis Signature Classics* (New York: HarperCollins, 2002), 94.

5. Mark Ellis, "Identical Twin Studies Prove Homosexuality Is Not Genetic," OrthodoxNet.com Blog, June 24, 2013, http://www.orthodoxytoday.org/blog/2013/06/identical-twin-studies-prove-homosexuality-is-not-genetic/.

6. Bryan Fischer, "No, Marco, Homosexuals Aren't Born That Way," *NE News Now*, April 20, 2015, http://onenewsnow.com/perspectives/bryan-fischer/2015/04/20/no-marco-homosexuals-arent-born-that-way.

CHAPTER 13: ESSENTIALS FOR HUSBANDS AND WIVES

1. Ed Wheat and Gloria Okes Perkins, *Love Life for Every Married Couple: How to Fall in Love, Stay in Love, Rekindle Your Love* (Grand Rapids, MI: Zondervan, 1980), 152-153.

2. Emerson Eggerichs, *Love and Respect: The Love She Most Desires; The Respect He Desperately Needs* (Nashville, TN: Thomas Nelson, 2004), 11.

3. Dr. James Dobson, *Bringing Up Girls: Practical Advice and Encouragement for Those Shaping the Next Generation of Women* (Carol Stream, IL: Tyndale House, 2010), 29.

CHAPTER 14: THIS MEANS WAR

1. *The Best American History Book in the World: All the Information You Need to Know without All the Stuff That Will Put You to Sleep*, Eric Burnett, ed. (New York: iUniverse, 2003), 205.

2. C. S. Lewis, *The Screwtape Letters*, annotated ed. (New York: HarperCollins, 1996), xlviii.

CHAPTER 15: WAKE UP, SOBER UP, SUIT UP

1. Mike Berardino, "Mike Tyson Explains One of His Most Famous Quotes," *SunSentinel*, November 9, 2012, http://articles.sun-sentinel.com/2012-11-09/sports/sfl-mike-tyson-explains-one-of-his-most-famous-quotes-20121109_1_mike-tyson-undisputed-truth-famous-quotes.

2. Corrie ten Boom, *Not Good If Detached* (Fort Washington, PA: CLC Ministries International, 2012), PDF e-book.

3. Robert Greene, *The 33 Strategies of War* (New York: The Penguin Group, 2006), Kindle edition, part 1.

ABOUT THE AUTHOR

Greg Laurie is the senior pastor of Harvest Christian Fellowship in Riverside and Orange County, California. Harvest is one of the largest churches in the United States and consistently ranks among the most influential churches in the country. He recently celebrated forty years as the senior pastor. In 1990, he began holding large-scale public evangelistic events called Harvest Crusades. More than five million people have attended Harvest events around the world, and more than 476,000 people have registered professions of faith through these outreaches.

He is the featured speaker of the nationally syndicated radio program, *A New Beginning*, which is broadcast on more than seven hundred radio outlets worldwide. Along with his work at Harvest Ministries, he served as the 2013 honorary chairman of the National Day of Prayer and also serves on the board of directors of the Billy Graham Evangelistic Association.

He has authored over seventy books, including *Tell Someone; As It Is in Heaven; Revelation: the Next Dimension; As I See It; Hope for Hurting Hearts; Married. Happily; Every Day with Jesus; Signs of the Times; Hope for America;* and many more.

He has been married to Cathe Laurie for forty-two years, and they have two sons, Christopher, who went to be with the Lord in 2008, and Jonathan. They also have five grandchildren.